SALES JIU-JITSU

SALES
JIU-JITSU

THE SECRET **BLACK BELT** SYSTEM FOR CHAMPION **LEADERS**

ELLIOTT BAYEV
DANIEL MOSKOWITZ

LIONCREST
PUBLISHING

SALES JIU-JITSU
The Secret Black Belt System for Champion Leaders

ISBN   978-1-5445-1573-1 *Hardcover*
       978-1-5445-1572-4 *Paperback*
       978-1-5445-1571-7 *Ebook*

To David and Yani Gellman for introducing
me to the beautiful art of Jiu-Jitsu.

—Elliott

To my wife, Lara, for always believing in me and my
children, Hyla and Samara, for their support. To my
father for always pushing me to be my best self.

—Love, Daniel

CONTENTS

THIS IS NOT A BASIC SALES BOOK.

THIS IS A BOOK FOR SALES BLACK BELTS.

INTRODUCTION

Only old-school, outdated sales theories and philosophies frame sales as a "fight." Winning modern sales philosophy frames the sales engagement as cooperative, collaborative, and supportive. Current high-performing sales teams frame sales as a service, and this shift has been responsible for explosive growth within the organizations that adopt it. So why are we writing a book that's using fighting as a way to teach sales? Because there is an art that uses connection over aggression. In Brazilian Jiu-Jitsu there is no hitting—instead you look to connect with the opponent, to get close enough to them that you can predict, guide, and even control their movements. Taking out striking each other allows participants to give 100 percent without hurting each other. It allows for an engagement that's competitive, playful, cooperative, contested, supportive, and fun in the spirit of mutual benefit.

"The best athlete wants their opponent at their best."

—*TAO TE CHING*

Jiu-Jitsu shows you that if you *really* want to serve your sparring partner, you bring your best self—your greatest strategies, efforts, and techniques. The best thing they can do for you is to hold you to a high standard by giving you the best possible challenge. But none of this is antagonistic. After even the most competitive matches, challengers hug in mutual respect and appreciation.

If you have something worthy of high-caliber clients, you have a duty to use every ethical, effective best practice and strategy available to help you show them how much you can help them. You want high-caliber clients to challenge you with their toughest questions, requirements, and standards. Iron sharpens iron. Every "fight," every sales engagement, is a collaborative, galvanizing *mutual leveling up.*

There has been a revolution in martial arts over the last hundred years, created by the birth and rise of Brazilian Jiu-Jitsu (BJJ), which has consistently dominated when tested against any single martial art. BJJ has been the backbone of today's most intense and realistic combat sport, Mixed Martial Arts (MMA), most notably through the Ultimate Fighting Championship and ONE Championship organizations.

There is a reason Brazilian Jiu-Jitsu is so effective. It follows fundamental principles—which apply *everywhere* in life but are easy to see and tap into through such a physical practice. There are distinct phases of engagement, parallel dynamics, and strategies that we can take from physical engagements and apply to sales engagements.

Rather than try to glean actionable principles by analyzing the *physical* art of Jiu-Jitsu, however, *Sales Jiu-Jitsu* uses **The Jiu-Jitsu Success Formula**—a four-part system Elliott developed that outlines *the process of preparing for and winning Jiu-Jitsu competitions.* This formula for training for, engaging in, seizing, and learning from challenges can teach us about the *processes* for achieving success anywhere. **The Jiu-Jitsu Success Formula** uses a match or a fight as an analogy for any challenge we face in life. Sales Jiu-Jitsu applies that system to the sales engagement.

Through the study of success on the mats, this book teaches a system of proven success practices designed to help seasoned Black Belt salespeople become sales *champions*.

Using the language of Jiu-Jitsu and lessons from competition, we take an original approach to outline proven tactics, strategies, and standard operating procedures for developing world-class sales teams.

THE JIU-JITSU SUCCESS FORMULA

The Jiu-Jitsu Success Formula is built around four primary phases necessary for winning in competition:

- **Pre-fight**—what we do to prepare for a competition
- **Fighting**—the match itself
- **Winning**—the seizing of victory within the match
- **Post-fight**—what we do after the match, win or lose

As competition is the aspect of Jiu-Jitsu that most closely resembles a sales engagement, we can apply the same system:

THE SALES JIU-JITSU SYSTEM
- **Pre-fight**—what we do in advance of the engagement
- **Fighting**—the engagement itself
- **Winning**—the obtainment of victory (for both you and the client)
- **Post-fight**—what we do after the engagement, win or lose

Each of these phases has its own frameworks, philosophies, and strategies. To win consistently over time, it's important to study, understand, and master the components of each phase.

THE SALES JIU-JITSU SYSTEM

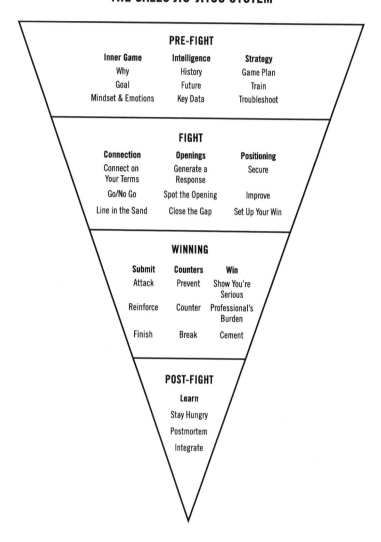

PRE-FIGHT

Inner Game	Intelligence	Strategy
Why	History	Game Plan
Goal	Future	Train
Mindset & Emotions	Key Data	Troubleshoot

FIGHT

Connection	Openings	Positioning
Connect on Your Terms	Generate a Response	Secure
Go/No Go	Spot the Opening	Improve
Line in the Sand	Close the Gap	Set Up Your Win

WINNING

Submit	Counters	Win
Attack	Prevent	Show You're Serious
Reinforce	Counter	Professional's Burden
Finish	Break	Cement

POST-FIGHT

Learn
Stay Hungry
Postmortem
Integrate

Apply any of the ideas in here to make an impact. Use them all together and the impact will be beyond belief. Make them a *habit*, a *routine*, and a *system* and the impact will be game-changing.

When implemented correctly, the Sales Jiu-Jitsu System will allow your sales team to take the leads you are already getting and convert them at a higher rate.

If you know you can help your clients, then every sales engagement is a battle where victory means you are able to help them solve a real problem they are facing, and defeat means you are not going to help them solve it. It's not about defeating *them*; it's about defeating *the forces that might get in the way of you helping them*. This means defeating the excuses that get in the way of you helping them solve their problem.

In every battle, you want to use your best weapon. That is now Sales Jiu-Jitsu.

SALES JIU-JITSU FOR TEAMS

It's easy to master sales strategies and processes when it's an individual who is selling. With teams, you need a system that makes maximizing revenues repeatable and predictable. This book gives you that system.

At the end of each chapter, we share visuals, action steps, worksheets, and checklists to help you implement the Sales Jiu-Jitsu System in your business. This is not a book to be read once and thrown on a shelf. It's a systems manual for developing a Black Belt sales organization.

Whether you are new to sales, a seasoned professional, or part of the elite echelon of world-class salespeople who are leading successful sales teams, this book will give you *the* competitive advantage in your industry and reward you for reading and taking action.

The system works together like a puzzle. Any one section on its own is powerful. All of it together will make you *unstoppable*.

WHO THE HELL ARE THESE GUYS?

Elliott is a second-degree Black Belt in Brazilian Jiu-Jitsu and has been studying, training, and competing in the art for more than twenty years, teaching for the last fifteen. He has competed at the highest levels, repeatedly representing Canada on the world stage, and has won dozens of medals and titles.

He spent a number of years in corporate sales before leaving the office life behind to focus on entrepreneurship and impact. Elliott has founded a number of business and impact projects over the last twenty years, in addition to running one of Toronto's most storied and successful martial arts academies, OpenMat Mixed Martial Arts. Elliott also runs Mastermind BJJ—a private Brazilian Jiu-Jitsu training program for elite entrepreneurs—and recently launched a Jiu-Jitsu education platform, BJJ101.tv, with courses for everyone from beginners to instructors (you can get a free copy of his beginner course, The BJJ Primer, by visiting www. BJJ101.tv/free-primer-download).

Off of the mats, his focus is impact. After honing the concept in private for a long time, Elliott recently launched Global Unity, a movement and a platform designed to help create a better world.

Daniel has been in sales for twenty-five years. In his long, successful career, he has worked in multiple B2B businesses and professional services industries, *personally* generating well over $30 million in B2B sales and heading up teams generating *tens of millions* of dollars per year.

Currently, Daniel is director of sales at Advance Your Reach, a company that helps individuals, entrepreneurs, and organizations leverage speaking on stages as a major client lead source. Daniel has helped to grow the organization from a seven-figure into an eight-figure company in two years.

HOW THIS BOOK CAME TO BE

Daniel, in the same circle of entrepreneurs as Elliott, saw a post on Facebook and came out to one of Mastermind BJJ's Toronto classes. He was not only taken with the art but recognized many of the lessons he had learned (and now teaches) in Elliot's approach to teaching the principles behind Jiu-Jitsu. Another Mastermind BJJ member half-jokingly proposed the idea of collaborating on a book, and what started as a wistful idea slowly grew into an unstoppable force. Through persistence and follow-through—an intense weekend-long sprint, months of back-and-forth, and more months of fine-tuning—this book came together. We're thrilled to be sharing it with you.

In each chapter you will find a section labeled "Jiu-Jitsu," written by Elliott and offset in italics and a section labeled "Sales," written by Daniel. The remainder of the book we wrote jointly.

We wish you, your organization, your team, and your clients the greatest heights of success. We believe the systems and processes herein can help you get Black Belt results regardless of the economy—even during a pandemic like the one we found ourselves in while writing this book.

A BRIEF INTRO TO BRAZILIAN JIU-JITSU

The following is a short excerpt from Elliott's intro to BJJ course, The BJJ Primer (to get free access, visit www.BJJ101.tv/free-primer-download).

You do not have to understand Jiu-Jitsu at all to get a lot out of this book, but it will give you a richer understanding to read this and the next section.

1. BJJ'S THREE-STEP SELF-DEFENSE FORMULA

Jiu-Jitsu started purely as a form of self-defense, answering the question: how do we stop a bigger, stronger, faster person who wants to hit or hurt us? It uses a three-step formula:

Step One: Close the Gap

From a safe distance

we protect ourselves

while we close the gap,

tying them up.

Step Two: Take Them Down

From here we take them down

to the ground, ensuring we remain on top.

Step Three: Establish the Mount

Stepping over their legs, we establish the mount position.

2. POSITIONAL DOMINANCE

Positioning is how we dominate. From a good position, things are easy; from a bad position, things are difficult. From the mount, for example, even the smaller, weaker person has a massive advantage.

Some positions offer unfair advantages.

3. NONVIOLENT SELF-DEFENSE: CONTROL VERSUS HARM

Rather than only teaching to hurt the opponent, Jiu-Jitsu teaches to control them. Once you have total control, you can hurt if you want, but you can also win peacefully.

You can control someone rather than try to hurt them.

4. PREPARING FOR WORST-CASE SCENARIOS

One of Jiu-Jitsu's strengths is *weakness*. We recognize that our plans will sometimes fail and thus dive into and answer the hard questions of what to do in tough spots—enabling us to prepare for them.

5. THE GUARD

In BJJ, we learn to fight from bad positions—on bottom. If someone wants to hit us while we are on our back, our best tools for protecting ourselves are our legs—the legs *guard* our head. Thus, we call any position where the top person is on the far side of the hips/legs *the guard*. It not only allows us to protect ourselves; it actually allows us to get *offensive*.

The guard can protect us from punches by controlling distance.

It also allows us to knock the opponent down and get on top, not to mention submit them (see #8).

6. PASSING THE GUARD

Because the guard is such a powerful tool, it is the one place the top person does not want to be. As such, "passing the guard," getting past the opponent's legs, is a major positional improvement and a vital skill for the top person. We can sometimes pass directly into the mount or, more often, we will pass and establish *side control*.

Controlling the legs,

we can use many methods to bypass them

and establish a dominant position.

7. POSITIONAL HIERARCHY

Jiu-Jitsu is often compared to chess. Step one is learning the chessboard—the field of play. There are four basic positions: the guard, side control, and the mount, all of which we've seen and *the back*—the fourth and most dangerous position. Because there is an offensive and defensive version of each, there are effectively eight positions. They can be ranked from best to worst:

THE POSITIONAL HIERARCHY OF BJJ

OFFENSE

The Back (Offense)   BEST POSITION

The Mount (Top)

Side Control (Top)

The Guard (Bottom)*

- -

DEFENSE

The Guard (Top)

Side Control (Bottom)

The Mount (Bottom)

The Back (Defense)   WORST POSITION

While we might consider being on top in guard a better position than being on bottom in a fight where the top person can punch, in the sport of Jiu-Jitsu, for the most part, only the bottom person has submission opportunities.

The back.

The mount.

Side control.

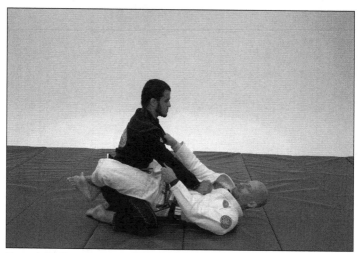

The guard (offensive).

8. SUBMISSIONS

The checkmate of Jiu-Jitsu, submissions are techniques that call an end to a friendly match. In self-defense and fighting situations, they actually enable us to subdue opponents. There are two types of submissions—joint locks and chokes. Joint locks take a limb past its natural range of motion causing injury, and chokes cut off either air to the lungs or blood to the brain. "Tapping out" is signaling to your training partner to let go of their hold—they have won. With few exceptions, only the person in the dominant position can submit the other.

Joint Locks

The armbar is a joint lock that hyperextends the arm.

Chokes

The rear naked choke cuts off the blood to the brain.

9. SPORT BJJ

Jiu-Jitsu teaches us how to overcome a stronger opponent. What happens, however, when they know what we know? This is where the chess game and the sport of BJJ emerges. Removing striking, sport BJJ pits athletes against each other in a test of skill. Submission brings ultimate victory and, in lieu of a submission, victory goes to the competitor with the most points, awarded for attaining dominant positions.

10. PULLING GUARD

As the guard is an offensive position—it enables both sweeps and submissions—it can be advantageous to be there. As such, one strategy we see in sport BJJ is "pulling guard," voluntarily choosing to be on bottom.

Pulling to a "closed guard."

GLOSSARY

Again, you don't need to know BJJ to read this book, but there may be some terms that are useful.

Belts

Belts in BJJ represent earned skill. There is a significant difference in skill between the belts. The order of belts is White, Blue, Purple, Brown, Black.

Bowing

A sign of respect and trust derived from Japanese culture. Often performed at the beginning and end of a match.

Escapes

An escape is a technique that either takes us from an inferior position to a better position *or* that enables us to get out of a submission.

Game

Game generally refers to one's skillset—the sum of their techniques, strategies, and proficiencies. "She plays a takedown-heavy game." "That White Belt is still developing their game," etc.

Gi versus No Gi

The gi (pronounced "gee") is the thick uniform shown in the photo on the next page. We use it to learn to not only escape when someone uses our clothes to control us, but to control and even choke people with it. In no-gi training, we cannot rely on the extra control and chokes offered by the gi.

Gi.

No gi.

Professor

The term used to address and refer to a BJJ black belt instructor.

Slap and Bump

The Jiu-Jitsu handshake, the slap and bump, is how most matches are initiated.

Submission

A joint lock or a choke, which requires the opponent to give up or face the threat of getting injured or going to sleep.

Sweeps

Sweeps are techniques that use the guard to turn the opponent over, allowing us to come on top.

Takedowns

Jiu-Jitsu's greatest strengths lie in the control it offers on the ground. As such, being able to take someone to the ground becomes important. Takedowns include throws, trips, tackles, and sweeps.

A double-leg takedown.

Tapping Out

Tapping our partner two to three times is how we signal that we want them to stop. It is the safety mechanism of BJJ, allowing us to end a match at any time.

Uke

Uke refers to our training partner. The uke is a vital role, as we must have a cooperative partner on whom to practice our techniques when we first learn them and a competitive partner to test them against.

PART I

PRE-FIGHT

If we fail to plan, we plan to fail.

—BENJAMIN FRANKLIN

It's important we understand what to do before, during, and after every fight. Our pre-fight work is going to set us up for success so that when it's time to engage, everything flows effortlessly. We must be prepared. This requires us to understand and master **inner game**, **intelligence**, and **strategy**. We must be on our own side, understand ourselves and the game *and* have a plan to win.

CHAPTER 1

INNER GAME

Yes, you will be engaging opponents. Yes, you will be fighting against outside forces. But everything you do will depend upon the strength of your inner position. Day to day, there will be many ups and downs. Your ability to stay the course will depend on the foundational work you do to set yourself and your team up for success *internally* so that no external challenges can derail you. There are three key areas—your **why,** your **goals,** and your **mindset and emotions.** Only by really understanding these can you position to win.

If you're a leader, you have to make sure that both you and your team have done this. It might seem basic, but basics win matches.

WHY

WHY: JIU-JITSU

I lay in bed, unable to hold my own head up.

I was twenty-three. I'd been an athlete most of my life. My whole identity was wrapped up in my physical prowess. Now I was trapped in bed, unable to lift my head without assistance.

My why brought me back from incapacitation.

On the first day of wrestling at the University of Toronto, the team was practicing "gut wrenches" techniques, where you grab the face-down opponent by the waist and roll them over to show control and dominance. I was the partner on bottom. The coach wasn't paying attention and, not having been shown how I was supposed to position myself, I tried to keep tight, putting my left cheek on the mat, thinking my partner was rolling me to the left. He rolled me to the right. My chin caught on the mat. I felt a sharp pain shooting down my neck and the rest of my spine as my head was turned nearly all the way around. Immediately, my thumbs were on fire, numb from the nerve pain shooting down my arm. Something bad had happened.

I tried to keep going, but the pain was overwhelming. Over weeks and months, it got worse. Eventually, while doing physiotherapy, my neck gave out completely. I collapsed on the floor. If I wanted to stand, I had to place my fingers on my collarbone and tent my wrist to create a shelf for my chin. I had had injuries before but not nearly as debilitating. So, I did what you are supposed to do—rest.

After the first hour, no change. Then the second hour, no change. Day one, no change...How long was this going to last? After a week in bed,

I was starting to question whether I'd ever be able to even walk free of pain, let alone fight again.

In those days and weeks, stuck in bed, I was forced to step back and really think about my path. Competing wasn't just about winning matches for me.

Years before, I had an idea that I felt would make a real impact. It felt like my life's purpose and still does. Not having come from money or having a technical background, I knew that in order to position myself to one day be able to launch it, I had to establish some kind of platform, some kind of following or name. The plan was to build a platform by spending a few years establishing myself in Jiu-Jitsu before venturing out into the impact world—and here I was, unable to even really stand.

With the mission in mind, I was determined to heal myself. Through weeks and months of pain and frustration, the vision of the impact I would one day make kept me going. I slowly found ways of minimizing the pain enough to start training again and eventually returned to competition, having since gone on to win at home and abroad. My why was the only thing that kept me in the fight long enough to win.

We are the engines of our own success. Without the right fuel, we do not perform. Our why is our fuel. On those days when you're exhausted and you don't feel like putting in the work, your why is what will help you push through. Aim high. The stronger our why, the more consistently we will show up, go the extra mile, and push through fatigue, pain, and discomfort.

WHY: SALES

Elite sales professionals are focused on maximizing commissions.

This is not a bad thing. You want sales professionals who like to make money. You want them to like to win. If they do, your company will thrive. Anything that pulls them off their game will affect their sales and the bottom line. You want to make sure that you and your reps have the necessary tools and support systems in place to quickly get back into the zone if ever they fall off. One of the most powerful tools that I have introduced in my teams is having a strong why.

I've heard it said that the mind is the greatest problem-solving machine, but you have to set it correctly. To set it correctly, you have to understand what your motivations are. The time in my life when this proved most salient was when I went on my weight-loss journey of losing 102 pounds. Years ago, I was 324 pounds, sick, and sick and tired of being sick. I would try to work out, thinking that would be the thing to do, but would come out exhausted, demotivated—and eating *more* because I had low blood sugar.

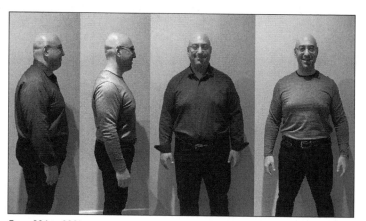

From 324 to 222!

My why came to me when my health coach said to me, "Write your own obituary; write the obituary of the life you want to have lived." I had never done anything like that, never taken a really hard, long view of life. I always approached life with a short-term view. In doing that exercise, I realized that I was telling the world that I hoped to live long enough to one day walk my daughters down the aisle. I had to call BS on myself. I looked at the business and life I wanted to create. How I was treating my body just wasn't in line with my goals; I wasn't going to live long enough to walk my girls down the aisle. In that moment I said to myself, "No, I *will* live long enough to walk my daughters down the aisle." It would be a hard journey to lose all that weight. If I was really going to do it, I needed a *why* with gravitas.

That day I got it.

I began a journey of ketogenic dieting and intermittent fasting. People talk about the "keto flu." Some people get it bad, and some people don't. I had probably one of the worst cases that anyone's ever heard of. It was seventy-two hours of a fever of 103 degrees. I had the shakes, chills, and headaches. I was vomiting and I had the runs. My wife came to my bedside and said, "Daniel, here is some bread. Just please eat the bread. You're killing yourself."

The old me would have easily accepted. "Hell no!" I told her.

The reason I had the fortitude to go through those seventy-two hours is that I had a strong enough why. I *did* want to live long enough to walk my daughters down the aisle, see them grow old and have kids. It *was* that important to me. It was beyond important. It pushed me to be able to go on. At the end of those seventy-two hours, I had my first piece of broccoli in twenty years, and it didn't upset my stomach.

I healed my body and I healed my *self*. Shedding the pounds became a positive-feedback loop. The more weight I lost, the better I felt, and the more motivating my why became. When you can find for yourself the why that matters most to you, it will give you the power to accomplish anything. Is it for family? Is it for your spouse? Is it *yourself*? Perhaps it's providing for other loved ones, like parents or kids. Or to make an impact in the world.

I had been stuck in the same position, battling my weight for over twenty years. Once I figured out my why, I did more work and saw more results in the next few years than I had in the past twenty. During the period where I lost all that weight, I launched a business that helped hundreds of entrepreneurs improve their sales, literally doubling their businesses. When I committed to my why, I had more success in that year than in my previous twenty because my why drove me to keep going when times were tough.

Discover and commit to your why.

A strong, clear, *articulated* why that you can check in with all the time allows you to come into every battle, every fight, every conversation, with a fire burning in you (and your team!) that shines brighter and more fiercely than your competitors'.

ACTION STEPS

We have created a Find Your Why worksheet for each person on your sales team to help find *their* why. We recommend introducing this worksheet by sharing *your* why and how it helps you day to day. Download at www.salesjiujitsubook.com/resources.

GOALS

GOALS: JIU-JITSU

Begin with the end in mind.

As 2007 came to a close, I started being able to move again. The pain was still there, but I could walk. Eventually, I was able to work out before finally returning to the mats.

A few months into my return, a friend asked when I was going to compete. "When I'm strong enough," I told him.

"If you keep waiting for the perfect time, you'll never do it," he replied. "Set the goal to compete, even if it's six months out." So I did.

Six months out was the 2008 IBJJF (International Brazilian Jiu-Jitsu Federation) Mundials—the world championship. Even though it seemed impossible to be ready in time, I wrote down the goal. It was amazing how, in addition to my larger why, which was a "someday" thing, a tangible goal brought a real focus and drive to my day-to-day training. Instead of training to avoid injury, I was training to win.

Inspired by the renewed vigor and focus, I wrote down a few "impossible" dreams to add a little extra fire, starting with "Abu Dhabi 2009." The Abu Dhabi Combat Club (ADCC) World Championship is the highest-caliber Jiu-Jitsu tournament in the world, the Olympics of Jiu-Jitsu. Only the best Black Belts in the world get invited to this no-gi tournament. The gi (pronounced "gee") is a traditional cloth uniform—no gi means competing in just shorts and a T-shirt. As a Purple Belt, barely able to train again, let alone compete, it was foolish to think winning was even possible. But I wrote it down. At the same time, I wrote down the name of my Jiu-Jitsu hero, Marcelo Garcia, setting the goal of one day training with him.

Eventually the Mundials came and, though I didn't win, I competed without injury—a win in itself, not to mention the technical and strategic lessons. Still, to think I might be able to compete in Abu Dhabi was downright preposterous.

*Then, toward the end of 2008, a new Abu Dhabi tournament was announced, the Abu Dhabi Pro. This was a gi tournament, and not only was there a Canadian qualifier, there was, for the first time, a mixed Purple Belt/Brown Belt/Black Belt division. The winner would be flown for free to represent Canada in Abu Dhabi. Even though it was still foolish for me, barely recovered and barely back to training, to believe I could compete and win, now it was at least **possible**.*

Whether I was to win or not, setting that "stretch goal" kept me forging ahead with training, focusing my energies and giving me the fire to push harder every day. Even if I didn't end up competing, I grew immensely from the extra push during that training camp.

Your why will inform a vision or an outcome you want—a dream. A goal is a dream with a date. Get specific; decide what you want and when. Aim high. It will push you further.

A strong why and a strong goal may not be everything you need, but without them, you won't have the fuel or focus to overcome the roadblocks between you and success.

GOALS: SALES

Being a sales Black Belt is about nuance. Rarely have I seen companies set both a benchmark and a stretch goal. When I was working at a conference company selling sponsorships, I took their goal and treated it as my benchmark. In year two, I was given a target of $400,000 and hit $1.4 million. But I didn't stop there. Setting a stretch goal, I was able to go from $1.4 million to $2 million over a three-year period. Recently, at Advance Your Reach we established a $7 million benchmark and a $10 million stretch goal—*and we beat the stretch goal!*

There's a direct correlation between sales goals and sales commission, plain and simple. Sales teams work toward a department goal, but they also need individual goals, revenue-based goals tied to their earnings—their commission. You can't manage what you don't measure, and in addition to sales goals, there are other key metrics worth setting goals around.

In my current role at Advance Your Reach, my team meets with prospects by video calls to enroll them into high-ticket workshops with packages ranging from US $10,000 to $35,000. Here are some metrics I watch on a weekly basis:

· Percent closing rate to number of calls/meetings (minus no-shows)
· Percent closing rate to number of unique clients spoken to that week
· Number of follow-up calls per week
· Average call time/meeting
· How long did rep versus prospect talk during a call?
· Number of down-sells
· Number of cross-sells/up-sells
· Current pipeline high–low next thirty and sixty days
· Sales by product category
· Number of video emails sent (I recommend a tool called www.bombbomb.com to send video emails)

If sales are low, one or more of these KPIs (key performance indicators) will be off. As sales leaders, we can't take our eye off of these—*ever*. By keeping them in front of the team through weekly meetings and one-on-ones, we can spotlight anytime they are out of whack—*and* turn them into a teaching opportunity. Anytime these metrics are off, we reset to get them back on track. We also want to understand *why* they fell off track. What's happening? Tracking these KPIs allows you to look deeper to figure out how to catch back up. Create a high-level daily dashboard and a deeper weekly scorecard that allow you to instantly take the pulse of your team.

Of course, when setting goals, you want to set up the team for success. If you set up a goal that is too outrageous, it can actually be a demotivator. That's not to say that a stretch goal is not in order. Like the Mundials and the "preposterous" goal of Abu Dhabi, having a benchmark goal *and* a stretch goal is key within any sales organization.

The benchmark is what you build your budget against. The stretch goal is what you're working toward. If your organization just had a $5 million year and you're looking to get moderate growth, you might set your benchmark goal to $7.5 million. At the same time, having a stretch goal of $10 million will get the team to push even harder. The key, in addition to setting the stretch goal, is to put a solid plan for achieving it in place; that way you will most likely surpass the benchmark if not reach the stretch. If you only put a plan in place to get to the benchmark, you'll never reach the stretch.

Aim for the stretch and use the benchmark as your measure of the team doing their job. Use the stretch goal—along with amazing rewards, constant motivation, rigorous, flexible planning, and thoughtful strategy—to reach beyond. I always tell my clients to use the benchmark to do their budgets, as it's safer, but also to have plans in place for when they reach the stretch. I also suggest keeping the running balance of both on your sales scorecard for the team to understand where the department is at all times.

Have your teams put these in place, and go kick butt.

ACTION STEPS

Set a benchmark sales goal for each month, quarter, and year. Then set a stretch goal that mirrors each month, quarter, and year. Then confirm that your sales and marketing strategies will get you to your stretch goal.

The best plan that I have found to help me as a sales director is to work with a marketing director to create a sales and marketing plan that lists out all the initiatives that are happening for the year. You can download a template that you can leverage at www.salesjiujitsubook.com/resources.

MINDSET AND EMOTIONS

MINDSET AND EMOTIONS: JIU-JITSU

*Competing for over two decades, I have had a number of breakthroughs throughout the years. Long before Abu Dhabi was even on the radar, I saw a massive jump in my performance and results after making one particular mindset shift. Early on, I would focus on what I didn't want to let my opponents do. By giving them my focus, my results were mixed. After reviewing video of some of my wins, seeing myself successfully pull off techniques, I shifted to focusing on myself. I came up with a "highlight reel" visualization technique. When I played a mental highlight reel of me pulling off my most kick-ass techniques over and over, nervousness turned to excitement and **results skyrocketed**.*

Abu Dhabi, however, was years later. Despite having had some strong mental tools, the prospect of entering a Purple/Brown/Black Belt division in the Abu Dhabi qualifier as a Purple Belt was intimidating. As I got on the train to Montreal, where the competition was being held, my confidence just wasn't there.

*Before I left, a friend gave me a book, **Mind Gym** by Gary Mack. It was the first time I had been exposed to the mental side of athletics, and it had a profound impact. An idea that really struck me was the **inner voice**. We all have an inner voice speaking constantly, and it's either a positive coach or a negative critic. Most people don't even realize there is a voice, let alone have control over it. The book offered new techniques and strategies for taking control of that voice. Finishing it before the end of the ride, I got off the train confident.*

I went to the tournament and won my first, close fight. Next, I faced a tough former training partner. When he left a small opening, I jumped on it, catching him in an armbar.

Eventually, I was in the finals against a guy who had easily overcome his previous opponents.

My mindset had been strong all day, but now I was fighting a more highly ranked opponent with a dangerous game. Between fights, a friend, Andrew McInnes, who was competing a few weight classes up, told me I had the best guard he had ever felt. Sometimes when your self-talk—that voice in your head—isn't quite there, having the right voice coming from the outside can be a huge boost.

At the beginning of the match, I took the guy down and was up 2–0. Midway, he caught me in a submission—a triangle choke.

The triangle choke—our knee cuts off blood to the brain through one carotid artery while the opponent's own shoulder cuts off the other, putting them to sleep.

Knowing it would be hard for him to finish the submission if I could get him up off the ground, I lifted him up. A year prior, I couldn't hold up my own head, and now I was holding up a 150-pound opponent on my shoulders. He let go and we scrambled, with me landing back on top. A game opponent, he was able to catch yet another submission, an omo

*plata shoulder lock, with just ten seconds left. I immediately jumped
over his head to defend and played it safe as the clock ticked down.
The match was over. I had won. Suddenly, **this foolishly impossible
pipe dream had come true.** I was going to Abu Dhabi.*

On the podium with the rest of team Canada. (Photo: Robert Strukelj)

*On the podium, minutes later, Andrew, who had also won his division,
told me he had moved to Florida to train with Marcelo Garcia and
invited me to come train with them. In the span of ten minutes, two
impossible dreams were coming true.*

On the last night of training with Marcelo in Florida. (Photo: Jimmy Lee Smith)

Having a why will fuel you to push your limits. Having big goals will focus your energies. But only with your mind in the right place will you be able to actually follow through in the midst of battle.

*Today, I coach all of my competitors not only to take control of their inner voice, but to see their own highlight reel. When I can get them to see all their best moves playing over and over, the nervousness they might feel is replaced by a burning excitement to make all those techniques happen. The quality of their performance skyrockets. The energy and emotion of seeing themselves kicking so much ass, not only makes competing more enjoyable for them—it gets **results**.*

MINDSET AND EMOTIONS: SALES

Entering a sales engagement with a clear mind and the right energy is key to your success. While many struggle with the inner critic, the elite sales professional often has mastered this (though not everyone on their team does). Beyond the inner game, every busy professional has so much outside noise to challenge them from being fully focused: getting the kids to school on time, having a spat with their partner, a parent not doing well, financial challenges, etc. There are always external factors that may throw the inner game off. On top of that, *internal* challenges will often arise. If yesterday's sales calls didn't go so well, you need a tool to help you bounce back. Similar to a competitor's highlight reel is the Power Book.

A Power Book allows you and your team to track and recall your sales wins. And not just the wins but the details behind them. When tracking your wins, capture the particulars of each challenge and how you overcame it. How did you originally engage the client? How did you overcome the obstacles they presented? How did you negotiate the contract?

In your Power Book, list all of them with vivid detail. Your book should be a quick reminder of your moments of brilliance. The particular jargon that got the client to understand how powerfully you could help them. The bonus features you threw in to help them off the fence. The original frame you set that made the whole rest of the engagement smooth and easy for both you and the client.

Reviewing these helps quiet the inner critic, take the external factors away, and enable you to get into the zone quickly. You and your team have successfully helped many clients—capture those successes.

The format matters less than the content. It may be physical, perhaps a journal. It may be online, as with a Google Doc or Evernote. I've seen corkboards with little recipe cards, each detailing a different successful sales situation. Whatever works.

Before you or your team enters into a sales engagement, you want to be fully focused and in a strong energetic and emotional state.

To do so, first go to your Power Book and review your moments of success. Next, do what you do to get into your peak energetic state. For some, this is taking a superhero pose:

The Superman.

Or

The Wonder Woman.

There is a clear difference between someone standing up confidently and someone hunching over meekly. How we stand, walk, and even sit informs how we think and how we feel. Do whatever feels right; stand up and take a position with your body that energetically makes you feel powerful. For some people, it's prayer; for some, it's yoga; for other people, it's rock music, rap music, or opera—whatever it is that fires you up.

Doing this, your team will feel energized and in the peak state to step on the mat and win. I do not know about you, but as a director of sales this excites me!

A great tip to share with your team: during my day, if I get a no, I give myself eight minutes. I allow myself eight minutes of reflection, eight minutes of thought, and time to go back to my Power Book, back to my routine before I step back onto the sales mat. The eight minutes is what I allow myself to recoup and reflect so that I don't carry any negative thoughts or any of the negative energy to the next conversation. I will ask myself, "What went right on this call? What could I improve?" Then, out loud, I say, "Thank you [NAME] for the lessons you just taught me, and thank you for the gift of time for saying no. Thank you."

Then I reset the clock and reignite that peak state by going back to my Power Book. When you can do this consistently, you will win without fail because losses become stepping stones rather than defeats. Give yourself the greatest opportunity to win the conversation and win the engagement by putting yourself in the best state possible.

Every team that I have ever introduced this to immediately increased their sales by at least 10 to 15 percent. Not only will it get quick results; it will have a compounding effect over time.

ACTION STEPS

Implement this for yourself, or share your own mindset and emotions techniques, then roll it out to your teams. We've created a template to get you started and get your team to be able to implement quickly. Download at www.salesjiujitsubook.com/resources.

CHAPTER 2

INTELLIGENCE

Knowledge is power. Before we start developing a plan, we must understand the field of engagement. You can have the right motivation and a focused mind, but if you are not knowledgeable and competent, you will fail. Once you have your inner game in place, you must study—both the environment and your opponents. We want to know what has worked **historically**, what new **trends** are emerging, and any **key information** about a particular opponent.

HISTORY

HISTORY: JIU-JITSU

You want to know what works.

Before you look to study the competition, study competition! If you have yet to compete, attend a competition. In either case, watch videos of fights. Always record and watch your own fights. What leads to victory? Analyze and find out.

There are no limits to the possible approaches we might encounter in a Jiu-Jitsu competition, but there are common strategies and techniques that tend to be more high-percentage than others. And while Jiu-Jitsu is evolving all the time, certain key staple approaches have been shown to work consistently over decades. Without understanding this, we might be the "better fighter" and still not win.

In Jiu-Jitsu, there are two ways to get a fight to the ground: you can take the opponent down, or you can "pull guard"—voluntarily (sometimes aggressively) choose to take the bottom position because of the offensive options it provides.

*In the late 2000s, people began analyzing the statistics of fights. What percentage of fights finished in a submission? Which submissions were most common? How did winning the initial interaction correlate to winning the match? It turned out that nearly **70 percent** of fights were won by the person who pulled guard. This is a powerful insight, whether you like to play from top or from bottom.*

For those who like to be on top, their plan, generally, is to take the opponent down, so they will dedicate much of their time practicing takedowns—techniques for throwing, tackling, tripping, or somehow otherwise putting the opponent on their back.

By studying the game and realizing that most people will pull guard, we can see that (a) we will not always have the opportunity to employ takedowns because the opponent may already have taken the bottom position, (b) we need takedowns that can work before the opponent has the opportunity to pull guard, and (c) we may want to employ techniques specifically to counter the ways in which someone would pull guard.

*Understanding this and other common practices empowers us to prepare for the likely eventuality of facing an opponent who pulls guard—or uses any other common high-percentage technique or strategy. If we want to win the game, we have to **understand** the game. This starts by studying what has worked so far.*

HISTORY: SALES

It's important to study our industry and what has been successful within it, but often overlooked are the winning techniques and strategies that are unique to that industry. One of the biggest problems within most sales departments is a lack of insight sharing. Every rep with wins under their belt has developed secret opening, engaging, and closing techniques that could be invaluable to their peers. Most balk at sharing these insights with others within the sales team for two reasons.

First, they feel they really *have* developed unique, effective strategies, and they fear that if they share them, they may risk their position and end up being reassigned to a new niche, effectively having to "start over."

The other reason reps are often averse to sharing is that they don't feel they understand why a particular approach worked, and they fear being "discovered."

As sales leaders, we need to document the knowledge from our reps and turn it into standard operating procedures (SOPs) of best practices that can be shared across the organization. This will allow us to study the "game" each rep plays and see which tactics work in a particular niche and which can be applied across multiple niches.

Documenting strategies that have won you business in your various industries, sectors, and niches is a key element to repeat success and cross-organizational learning. Creating a *niche-specific database* to capture the details of each approach and what happened to win the deal is something very few organizations do—and something that will take you and your team to the next level.

Each rep may take a bit of a different approach within each niche, but they all can win through sharing the details. If each rep documents these successes, everyone on the team can quickly learn what is working and duplicate that success. Understanding what has worked for your organization and in specific industries—and sharing that data—empowers each sales rep to be as effective and productive as possible.

In addition to the history of your reps, an important element to consider is the history of what a target company has done, especially if you're going after publicly held companies. You have an opportunity to read their shareholder reports and see over time how they make big decisions. You can use these insights to plan your approach.

ACTION STEPS

We have created a sample niche-specific database to get you started. You can customize the headings to your industry.

Headings:

- Why would each niche want your product?

- What is important to them?

- What pitches have worked in the past?

- Who were the decision makers?

- What was the average deal size?

- What product or what bundle of products were pitched and sold?

Be sure to allow access to your entire sales team, and consider giving marketing read-only access, as you'll collect interesting data for them to use to develop new campaigns that might just bring in more leads. Download at www.salesjiujitsubook. com/resources.

FUTURE

FUTURE: JIU-JITSU

Jiu-Jitsu is always changing. New techniques and strategies are constantly being developed.

Years ago, a new, powerful technique started to gain popularity in gi competition, the berimbolo. Seemingly impossible to stop, it was a specialized move for basically teleporting to the best position. With it, you go from the bottom, the guard, all the way to the most dominant position—"the back" (tightly controlling someone from behind). While there are many other techniques for accomplishing the same objective, this did it in a way that seemed impossible to stop. It was not uncommon to see Blue and Purple Belts taking the backs of Black Belts by using it.

Similarly impactful in no gi, leg submissions—joint attacks against the knees and ankles—have been in vogue in recent years. Rather than play the traditional games of either taking the opponent down or pulling guard in order to get on top, leg lockers would often pull guard just to be able to entangle the opponent's legs, which can lead directly into a submission—even with a significant size or rank difference.

When innovations like these emerge, you must study them, both so you can use them and so you can counter them. Keeping a finger on the pulse of trends is key. What is changing in your field of battle? What trends are emerging that you need to be aware of?

FUTURE: SALES

You need to know what is happening within each of the niches you service. You must know the future trends that you're looking for, what's happening in the economy, and what's happening in politics. Are your niches affected by any new legislation? Is there anything new that's coming down the pipe, and what will be the effect on the industry?

After the 2008 crash, for example, new laws added new requirements to financial firms. Many companies within the financial sector had to have off-site backup locations to protect data and provide business continuity in case of disruption. They had to make investments in that infrastructure in order to have their data, their company, and their people continue to run in the event of an emergency, like an earthquake, riot, or fire.

Data centers started to use extra server space to create these continuity locations to service small and medium-sized organizations. It was great recurring revenue for them, as it was dormant space they otherwise didn't use. I know this because I sold corporate video to one such firm that was ahead of the curve.

Knowing what legislation is coming and what rules are being implemented can allow you to spot opportunities. Does your solution provide any kind of competitive advantage that will actually protect somebody from a trend that is about to happen?

If you're in a position to know that a recession is coming or that something like COVID-19 is likely to trigger another pandemic, what product or service do you have that can help somebody in other industries save their market share or even increase their market share in that particular environment? If you know that a recession is coming, you'll be knocking on the doors of people in advance, because these things don't pop up overnight.

You can knock on those doors ahead of time and be ahead of the curve. Be the first to offer a solution for a problem that they know is coming as opposed to one they already have. Your solution to a problem they already have is fine. If you can offer a solution to a problem they know is coming and you can be first to offer it, you're able to dominate in areas where others are inactive or, at best, reactive. You're *proactive*.

Turn what looks like chaos and no opportunity into an opportunity. (Sometimes the future opportunity lies in data you get from your most raving fan clients—which is good reason to pay attention to chapter 4 on connection later in this book.)

During the first year I sold sponsorships for a conference company, I was finding my way in a new industry. I was given a goal of $250,000 and hit $300,000. They were happy, but I was still looking for the keys to higher revenues. At the start of my second year, I had a call from my biggest client, Janet, who asked me for help. She said, "My boss just gave me $50,000 to spend on US-based conferences, and they are all promising the world. You always explained the value of your sponsorship deals so well and delivered on them every time. Can you help me?" I said, "Of course, but first let me ask you a question. If I could *teach* you how to evaluate any sponsorship deal that came your way, would that be valuable to you?" She said, "Hell yes!" I proceeded to help her, and this led me to altering how I sold sponsorships forever. I developed a forty-five-minute presentation that I could deliver over the phone. (This was before Skype, so I would email the deck and say, "Next slide," while taking them through it over the phone.)

I would call up and say, "I have been providing this new presentation to all my existing clients to teach them how to evaluate any sponsorship opportunity that comes across their desk." I named some big clients who found it very beneficial. Then I'd ask, "Would you be interested in scheduling a presentation for yourself and your team?" At the end of the presentation the common response was "Best forty-five minutes I spent all quarter. What sponsorship opportunities do you have for me?"

Providing key information that was not available anywhere else *before* I asked for any business is what allowed me to go from $300,000 to $1.4 million in one year. It was a game changer for me, and I have taken this concept with me to each organization.

ACTION STEPS

We have created a cheat sheet to help you research future trends. Have your sales team do the exercises on it individually, then come together as a team to review and create strategies to create a first-mover advantage. Discuss whether any of your key clients have asked for help that is within your area of expertise. If so, what was it, and how could you turn that into a pre-sales engagement tool? Download atwww.salesjiujitsu-book.com/resources.

KEY DATA

KEY DATA: JIU-JITSU

Sometimes you know who you're fighting; sometimes you don't. When you do, you can sometimes find information on them; other times you can't.

You might already know who they are. You may have fought them before or know someone who has. Sometimes you get updated information on fight day—you see them compete against someone else before you face them. That's key information about how they like to play—insight that may help you win.

Years ago, a Black Belt named Majid Hage started choking people with a baseball bat choke **while they were past his guard***—the vast majority of chokes only work while you still have the opponent in your guard. He was choking them* **unconscious***. If you know an opponent's game, you can spot danger and avoid their strengths.*

The baseball bat choke—one of the rare chokes that works without requiring the opponent to be in front of you.

Jiu-Jitsu is the art of adaptability. Yes, you go in with a certain plan, but you have to mold it to the circumstance and the opponent. I may prefer to take my opponents down and attack from the top, but if I am facing a high-level wrestler or judo player, both known for their ability to take opponents down, it may be wiser to pull and attack from guard.

Use every insight you have about each opponent and adapt your plan accordingly.

KEY DATA: SALES

I did five minutes of research using the $5R + 5M = C$ formula I describe below before starting a meeting with a potential client. On YouTube, I found that they had over three hundred videos, and it was there I hit pay dirt. I saw that the CEO of the company had ridden an elephant on stage for a user conference. And I thought, *That's it. Nobody does that unless there's a story there.*

I went in to meet the CEO. First thing I said with a lot of excitement was "Joe. Joe! I am so excited to have this conversation with you today. I've been looking forward to it all week."

"Really? Okay. Tell me why."

"All week, I've been so looking forward to this. You just have to tell me, man. What was it like to ride Dumbo between your legs because I'm super interested. What permits did you need, and was it a poop machine? Tell me; I have no idea."

Total laughter. All the guards came down. We connected. We geeked out on that for five minutes, then moved into the meeting. And I would not have known if I didn't have the discipline to do this simple five-minute check every single time. I wouldn't have been in a position to win the agreement.

To avoid making any assumptions when you look at your opponent, you need data. If you take a step back and actually get that intelligence, you can approach a situation much differently. The other part of that is creating it as a standard operating procedure (SOP), which you always do. As I have learned as a director of sales in many organizations, it's one thing to have a process and another thing to ensure that it's always being followed.

The Connection Formula

$5R + 5M = C$

Good strategies are based on good information. One of the most successful key data strategies that I teach my teams is what I call the Connection Formula:

$5R + 5M = C$

It's five points of research (R) that you need to do before you *step onto the mat* with a sales prospect so you can, during the first five minutes (M) of the call, connect (C) and build true rapport.

This applies to both one-on-one conversation and a boardroom full of people. If you can, you want to know who those folks are going to be before you enter the room. Spend one minute looking them up on each of the following platforms:

- Google
- Facebook
- YouTube

- LinkedIn
- The company website

You're looking for something you can geek out about with them for five minutes. This will feed into the beginning of your sales conversation, which we are going to discuss next. But if you're able to find that one thing that you can genuinely connect about with that person, it's a game changer. It could be that you went to the same school. Or you grew up in the same town. Religion. Kids. Married. Hobbies. Sports. Whatever it is, find the thing that you could genuinely geek out about with that person for five minutes.

When you find that data, you'll be in a position to have an instant connection and create real rapport. Remember—people buy from people they like and with whom they *connect*. This is an amazing SOP to have your team adopt and build into five minutes of their calling schedules.

There is a sixth source of data that is a total ninja hack. If you happen to know someone connected to your prospect, you can ask them for the data you need.

The key is having this as a systematic approach that you roll out to your entire team, allowing those kinds of moments to happen day in and day out instead of stumbling around asking questions to try to find connection.

No, you *make* this happen. You create it by doing the due diligence *before* you step onto the mat.

ACTION STEPS

We've created a tool in our resource center to help your team know what they're looking for in each of these areas so they can create an instant connection on their next sales call. Download at www.salesjiujitsubook.com/resources.

CHAPTER 3

STRATEGY

Now that you have your intel, it's time to use it to develop your strategy. This is the heart of your Jiu-Jitsu. Can you solve the problems you're been presented with?

Anytime I have a student compete, the first question I ask them is "If it goes perfectly, what does that look like?" That helps them develop a framework, a skeleton of what outcome they want optimally—their **game plan.**

Once you've got a game plan, you must **train.** Put your theory to the test. You may game-plan to take an opponent down, but if it doesn't happen in training, you have to recognize that and adapt. Practice shows you your strengths and weaknesses—it shows you *reality.*

Use reality. Face your problems. If something isn't working, **troubleshoot** by focusing on where you struggle. Any problem you encounter points the way to your next level of learning.

GAME PLAN

GAME PLAN: JIU-JITSU

Competing to win is trying to impose your desired reality on the world. A game plan is the story that outlines that desired reality.

How does the fight start? Are you letting the opponent dictate it? How are you finishing the fight? From what position? How did you get there? The game plan is your articulated vision of victory. It helps you know what to look for on the mats and gives you something specific to visualize.

I like to build my game plan around my strengths, independent of the opponent. For example, I pull guard; I sweep in this particular way. I pass their guard; I finish (submit them) that way. It's important to know what reality you're trying to create.

But if you only do that, you're not prepared for when the person, say, pulls guard first. The challenge is—how do you create an offensive game plan and still be prepared for contingencies?

Quantum Strategy

*The night before the 2010 Abu Dhabi World Championship Canadian Trials, which I had won the year before, I developed a new method for focusing on my optimal game plan while **simultaneously** preparing for alternate possibilities—what I call Quantum Strategy.*

Typically, I might map out a simple game plan linearly, top to bottom:

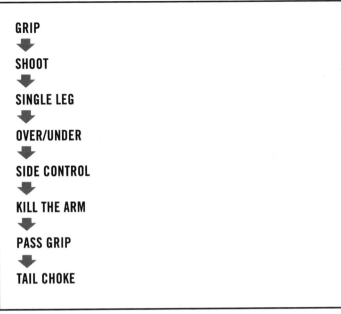

GRIP
⬇
SHOOT
⬇
SINGLE LEG
⬇
OVER/UNDER
⬇
SIDE CONTROL
⬇
KILL THE ARM
⬇
PASS GRIP
⬇
TAIL CHOKE

In the primary game plan, I get a grip on the opponent's collar and shoot for a single-leg takedown. Once they are down, I pass their guard with an over/under pass, finishing in side control. From here, I kill the arm, pass the tail of my own gi to my cross-facing hand, and finish with a tail choke.

Next, I asked, "What if things go wrong? What if the opponent pulls guard before me?" How do you represent both "realities" on the same page? With a divider. The "/" line represents a different "reality" in which something happens other than the intended game plan. The arrow represents a sequence of events that returns us to the original game plan.

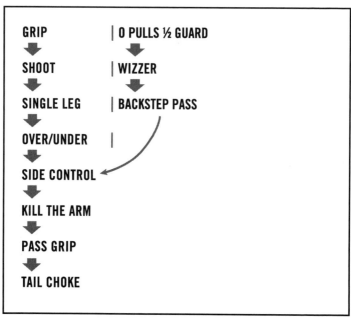

GRIP | O PULLS ½ GUARD
⬇️   ⬇️

SHOOT | WIZZER
⬇️   ⬇️

SINGLE LEG | BACKSTEP PASS
⬇️

OVER/UNDER |
⬇️

SIDE CONTROL ⬅
⬇️

KILL THE ARM
⬇️

PASS GRIP
⬇️

TAIL CHOKE

Using the "|" line to create an "alternate reality," I plan for when things go wrong. If, as I go to get a grip, the opponent pulls half guard, I shut down their initial attacks with a wizzer. From there, I backstep in order to pin them in reverse half guard, before passing, again landing in side control, and continue with the original game plan.

In this way, you could go many "layers deep" mapping out possibilities.

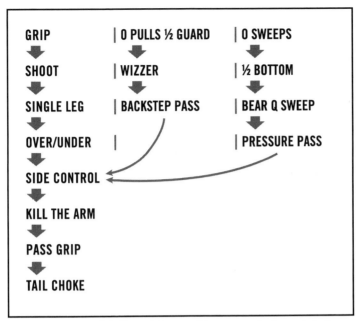

GRIP	O PULLS ½ GUARD	O SWEEPS
⬇	⬇	⬇
SHOOT	WIZZER	½ BOTTOM
⬇	⬇	⬇
SINGLE LEG	BACKSTEP PASS	BEAR Q SWEEP
⬇		⬇
OVER/UNDER		PRESSURE PASS
⬇		
SIDE CONTROL		
⬇		
KILL THE ARM		
⬇		
PASS GRIP		
⬇		
TAIL CHOKE		

If, as the opponent pulls half guard, they are able to sweep, forcing me to half guard bottom, I use the Bear Quitugua sweep, getting back on top, again in half guard. Using a pressure pass this time, I again finish in side control and continue with the original game plan.

And so on. This helped me feel extremely well prepared. In my first fight against a Brown Belt from Montreal, he pulled half guard exactly as I'd mapped out in my contingency plan the night before. I responded as intended. I remember smiling to myself for a moment at how perfectly the moment mirrored the game plan up to that point. The fight didn't go entirely as planned—he was quite good—but the preparedness gave me the confidence to impose myself on him and ultimately take his back and choke him out.

Moments before the choke. (Photo: Robert Strukelj)

*In the semi-finals of the 2010 Abu Dhabi Trials, I knew the opponent was tough, so I went to my "A game": I jumped closed guard. His posture was better than anyone I had **ever** felt. Unable to break him down, I opened my guard and swept him with my "B game": my spider guard. He ended up getting injured in the sweep, so I won the fight by default and was on my way to the finals.*

Yes, you must develop a solid, clear plan. But everyone does that. Go beyond and plan for contingencies.

Reality is just branches of possibility. Take control.

GAME PLAN: SALES

Elite sales teams have game plans in the form of sales playbooks, which are comprised of major paths that the sales conversations can take in order to anticipate them. You prep by role-playing these scenarios; however, for this exercise to be useful, you must first choose *what* to role-play. I recommend looking at the match and plotting between twenty-five and fifty different scenarios in advance, including all the countermoves that get you to the yes, *before* stepping onto the mat.

These mind maps only get better with time, and soon you will walk into all conversations knowing the outcome about halfway through.

Some of them might be far-fetched, but experience will tell you which are more likely. When you train your team to be disciplined and role-play consistently, they'll have zero anxiety or trepidation if the conversation takes an unanticipated turn. Even a surprise direction may be very similar to one they mapped out. The goal is to have them come in prepared enough to be able to say, "Well, I hear that all the time, and let me tell you how we've dealt with that problem" or "This is how the solution works here."

The more complicated your product or service and the greater the investment, the more variations you want to map out. When it's a $25,000 to $1 million sale, twenty-five to fifty scenarios tend to cover most possibilities.

When I sold conference sponsorships, we had an opportunity with a trading organization. They had requested a meeting. I knew that they had sponsored the year before and had sponsored some specific events at the conference. As well, I knew, based on some intelligence, that one of the people I was to meet with was French Canadian. I came up with a number of scenarios that embedded some French cultural elements. I devised four different variations on the sponsorship opportunity, three of them with varying degrees of a Paris theme, including a fifty-foot-tall Eiffel Tower made of ice, a mime, and singing characters guiding people to a lunch with a Paris-themed lunch menu.

They absolutely loved the cultural angle and signed up for double the amount that they had spent the year before. I had more straightforward backup plans if they didn't like it, but I came into the conversation with the key data that I needed in order to think as the client thought and future-cast a dream outcome and a game plan for getting there.

ACTION STEPS

Map out your perfect outcome. Imagine your perfect sale. What does that look like? Write it out.

Once that's down, start to show the different outcomes and how you'd respond.

With your current top prospects, create a mental movie of you executing against your plan. This is just like the highlight reel that allows you to see yourself winning over and over.

Quantum strategy: then take this highlight reel and boil it down to simple little one-liners for each contingency that you can fit on a cue card: the Paris-themed lunch, option one, two, three.

Use the Sales Jiu-Jitsu System as your base map, then create scenarios from there. Download at www.salesjiujitsubook.com/resources.

TRAIN

TRAIN: JIU-JITSU

*It's one thing to have an idea of what you want to have happen, but unless you actually test that plan, you don't know how effective it will be. What truly separates Jiu-Jitsu from other arts are not only the techniques but the **training methods**. Japanese Jiu-Jitsu, for example, uses many of the same techniques as Brazilian Jiu-Jitsu, but they train in a rote fashion—an attacker comes at us in this prescribed way and we respond with a set of techniques while they effectively cooperate. In BJJ, by contrast, we initially cooperate when being introduced to a technique so we can build the muscle memory, but we then try to use our techniques against each other with varying degrees of resistance. It's getting used to this resistance that makes us effective in competition and in self-defense, where doubtlessly opponents will resist.*

Once you have a game plan, you must put it to the test.

Years ago, when I was a Purple Belt, I was getting ready for the No-Gi Pans, one of the bigger no-gi tournaments on the East Coast. My game plan involved pulling guard, attacking the back.

This is a classic game that has worked for me hundreds of times in training and quite a few in competition. But as I trained with higher-level opponents, it stopped working. As they became familiar with my game, they came up with ways to stop it. This was initially frustrating, but that's what we want. We want weaknesses exposed. If there is a hole in our approach or plan, far better to have our partners shine light on that in training than get exposed in competition.

Train your game plan and see what really works and what doesn't.

JITA KYEOI: ON BEING A GOOD "UKE"(PARTNER)

*Uke, from the Japanese word **ukeru**, which means "to receive," is a term given to our training partner, the person with and on whom we practice our techniques. It is a vital role, and thus it's important both that we have a good uke when practicing and that we know how to **be** a good uke when it's our partner's turn. Jita Kyeoi is a term coined by Jigoro Kano, the founder of judo, to describe how two partners should be working together; loosely, it means "mutual prosperity and benefit," or simply "win-win."*

*The idea is that your partner needs someone giving the right energy to practice their moves on—without that, you cannot really develop skill. It's not uncommon to see a beginner unversed in this concept trying to "fight back" during technical practice, defeating the purpose. Technical practice is cooperative. Yes, **real** resistance is what makes BJJ so powerful, but the level of that resistance has to be appropriate to the particular type of training. A good uke will adapt their energy and resistance level to match and challenge their partner.*

TRAIN: SALES

"As the Buddhist saying goes," Simon Sinek has said, "how you do anything is how you do everything." This goes for training as well. You need to be as disciplined about practicing for your sales engagements as you are about closing them. Give space and dedicate time to allowing your sales team to practice, as you only have one chance to make a first impression.

Find the areas that move the needle most in your clients' organizations. When looking at an upcoming opportunity, I will normally review the top five to ten scenarios and work on training those that are the most likely to come up.

Training has served me well on so many occasions. My team

was once getting ready to pitch to an insurance company, and during the deck training a team member said, "I was not at the meeting where you decided that direction. Explain how you arrived at that decision." It was a great point we had not planned for. So, we embedded the first deck, hidden, into our new presentation so we had what we needed to fill in the blanks of anyone on the client's side who had missed the first pitch meeting.

This was right on the money; we had the exact same question come up from someone new who joined the pitch meeting. We said, "We thought that this might come up," then revealed the slides and took them through the earlier deck. It made us look like rock stars, our company champion was happy, and we got the deal. This never would have happened if we had not trained.

ACTION STEPS

Schedule weekly training for the next three months. Have your team look at the next opportunity and practice the top five to ten scenarios for it. Log these sessions so you can go back to them during your postmortem, which we cover in part 4, Post-Fight. You can download our Sales Training Session Logs at www.salesjiujitsubook.com/resources.

TROUBLESHOOT

TROUBLESHOOT: JIU-JITSU

When you actually practice "live"—fully resisting and improvising— you encounter problems. Things don't work out as planned. One powerful and seldom discussed aspect of Jiu-Jitsu is troubleshooting, a cooperative form of training in which you and your partner go into the "laboratory" of a position.

You have them slowly attack with a technique that you have trouble defending, giving you the chance to test different responses. You stop, discuss, get ideas from them, and test those. You are both trying to solve and improve—Jita Kyeoi. When things go wrong, ask what else you could do instead—and then, of course, what the opponent could do in response.

You might not work on a weakness. You might have a strength that you want to tighten up further. How will they react to this attack? What are the ways you can shut those counters down? You may be switching from gi to no gi and need to figure out how to adapt your game.

We must take control of our own learning and development. Learn what to do. Get the information you can and figure out the rest.

In the example from the previous section, Train, training showed me that there was a weakness in my game plan—good opponents were able to shut down my pendulum sweep. It seemed there was no way to address their counter and I was tempted to give up on the whole game plan.

Mental Jiu-Jitsu

Once you've trained for a few months, you will have gotten to see so many ways of getting out of situations you might at first think were *inescapable. Because in Jiu-Jitsu there is a solution for every problem, you realize that every problem is really Jiu-Jitsu asking you **how do you solve that problem?***

Mental Jiu-Jitsu is turning problems into questions. Using the specifics of the problem to ask what a solution to this type of problem would look like and tinkering to find one that fits.

*After experimenting in the position, I came up with a new technique, the **belly bump**, that not only knocked them over, allowing me to get on top, but put me right into position to finish the fight.*

After quickly tapping my first opponent with an armbar—one branch of the game plan—I tried the same game on my second opponent. Savvy, he knew the counter that would shut down my basic game. Not only was I able to use the belly bump on him, I used it twice, winning the fight, eventually taking silver in the division.

From the podium at the IBJJF No-Gi Pans, 2009. (Photo: Unknown)

*If I had not developed a game plan and **trained** that game plan against resisting opponents, I wouldn't have found out where my weaknesses were. Troubleshooting and using Mental Jiu-Jitsu enabled me to come up with new and better answers to problems I thought were unsolvable.*

Recognize the problems you keep running into and brainstorm and test multiple possible solutions to them. You will come up with new, innovative solutions.

TROUBLESHOOT: SALES

If you're presenting as part of your pitch, it's one thing to practice it in a vacuum, in the safety and comfort of your office. It's another thing to do it in front of a live person who will ask questions, stop you, and throw you something out of left field—somebody who's challenging you in the moment, giving you resistance. Training in a vacuum will not help you. It gives you the robotic way of doing a sales conversation, which is just fiction. It's not reality. The reality very rarely goes to plan. It usually goes to one of your alternate plans. You'll never know how to make those shifts and those changes unless you have uncovered pivot points through troubleshooting.

Develop a culture that encourages cooperative, challenging role-play within your organizations. Set up opportunities for your salespeople to get feedback not just off of sales conversations after they have happened, but *before they ever get in there.* They need an environment in which to do that. Often, organizations will create teams that allow for space to have semi-private sparring sessions.

Semi-private sessions take place within the sales team, where the team can play a little bit with various scenarios and "spar" them out. That's the key to being a proactive sales team as opposed to a reactive one. Many organizations are simply set up as a reactionary model where their calls are reviewed, feedback is given, and expectation of change happens. Sometimes a rep is given a scenario and they have to record a response. Again, this is mechanical and *not* a real-time scenario. Elite skill comes from having an intelligent sparring partner on the other side who actually lobs you objections, challenges you, and asks you questions.

That's intense training—trial by fire. Iron sharpens iron. Even if the scenario doesn't come up, it's very valuable training. One of the Navy SEALs sayings is "Get comfortable being uncomfortable." This will prep you for sales moments that will challenge you emotionally.

The new objections that troubleshooting uncovers are amazing. Often, you will find the objection that you didn't think about. Logging these is critical. Create a best practice where objections are logged into an objections database for everyone at the organization to access. They can go to the objections database before they start training and pull some to throw at you. The objections database is fed from two places: training and live scenarios.

An objections database not only can be used by sales, it also can be used by marketing. When you market to people's objections, you never have to deal with them during the sale.

Mental Jiu-Jitsu for Sales

Once you have identified objections, you must develop responses and add those responses to the objections database. You are likely already aware of tons of responses to common objections—add those to the database first. If responses come up in troubleshooting, great, record them, but if you get stumped, ask, "What *would* solve this problem? What *would* make the client happy, come in on budget, and inspire them to stretch that budget and make our internal champions look great? It's important to identify problems, but then you have to solve them. Troubleshoot, and when new objections come up, Mental Jiu-Jitsu your way to solutions.

ACTION STEPS

Train!

Set up a buddy system. Set up a time for intense training and make sure to have a system for recording it so you can capture any *ahas*. Use the objections database as a way of communicating what you come up with to the rest of the organization.

The objections database captures the objection and logs the solution. Here are examples of ways to log:

- New ways we're countering old objections

- What you have seen that's worked in this industry or niche

- Phrasing that has been successful with clients

- Setting up your objections database: download a sample at www.salesjiujitsubook.com/resources.

- After every role-play session, identify any objections you did not have answers for and schedule a time to use Mental Jiu-Jitsu to ask, as a team, how you can answer that objection in a win-win way.

PART II

FIGHTING

This is the Art of War.
It's the most important skill in the nation.
It is the basis of life and death.
It is a philosophy of survival and destruction.
You must know it well.

—SUN TZU, *THE ART OF WAR*

This is the art of fighting. It is a skill. It can be developed; it can be broken down and picked up one piece at a time. Fights can be won. This is how.

Now that we have prepared, it's time to engage. It's time to apply what we've practiced. It's time to fight. As with our preparation, there are phases of the engagement. First, we must **connect** with the opponent, **see the openings** they present, before finally **positioning** ourselves to win.

CHAPTER 4

CONNECTION

Fights begin with an initial engagement. How we engage matters. The biggest tree in the world grows from the tiniest sprout. Big problems start from little problems. If we do not win the initial engagement, if we just let the engagement happen or let the opponent dictate where the fight takes place, we take the risk that the tide starts turning against us. We must dictate how we **connect, recognizing which situations are acceptable** and which ones are not, while also **recognizing what we need to press forward.**

CONNECT ON YOUR TERMS

CONNECT ON YOUR TERMS: JIU-JITSU

Connect on your terms. Control the fight. Take control by dictating how you want the engagement to begin.

*If you have a dangerous guard, but you know your opponent does too, it might be wise to choose to get to the bottom first so they cannot play from their strongest position. Lighter-weight competitors in particular often have good guards and you will frequently see **both** competitors vying to get to the guard first. In the 2018 Ontario Open, one of my athletes, Rodrigo Goncales, was competing in the light-featherweight Purple Belt division. Everyone in that division has a good guard and, even if you are better overall, letting them play to their strengths is risky. Rodrigo has an extraordinarily dangerous guard and, as a Blue Belt, he would sometimes let the opponent dictate how the match started. Not this time. In every fight, he pulled guard **first** and submitted everyone within about a minute, taking gold. He's now a Brown Belt.*

In the finals of the 2017 Rickson Gracie Cup in New York, I faced an opponent from a team called 10th Planet. While I trust my guard passing, they are a school known for having good guards, and so it seemed wiser to avoid the opponent's strengths by pulling guard myself. I did so aggressively at the beginning of what turned out to be a close fight. I won the match and ultimately the division, but it could easily have gone the other way if I had let the opponent dictate the playing field.

With the great Rickson Gracie after taking double gold. (Photo: Fay Mavrea)

Starting with an initial advantage changes everything, and having insights about the opponent or field of opponents can help you both frame the fight and start a step ahead.

"Be first!" is a command shouted by coaches everywhere, because whoever dictates how the fight starts begins with a massive advantage. Dictate where the fight takes place. Be first.

CONNECT ON YOUR TERMS: SALES

When I'm conducting call reviews on my team, one of the first things on my checklist is "Did they establish true rapport before moving on in the call?" If this is not established, the reps will rarely make the sale. When I talk about the fact that you need to make a real human-to-human connection, it's not some fluffy concept or me being a softie. It's hard-core practical. You must treat sales as a service. People need problems solved, and if you believe you can solve a problem for them, then it's your duty to show them that you are the one to do so. People *only* buy from people they like and connect with. To be of service and help them solve their problem, you *must* connect with them. If you don't do this step, your prospect may tragically never solve their problem—or, worse, they may sign up with someone else who won't actually help them.

Make a human-to-human connection. Too often, salespeople are taught to ask one small personal question and then get into the "real reason for your call." This can hurt rapport by depersonalizing the call. It's not an actual connection unless we put something on the table. Your reps must get a little personal in order to connect with the prospect.

In a fight, you're chest to chest, cheek to cheek. You're in each other's space. When you can make it as personal in sales, it puts you into another category. So, with our five pieces of key data in the Connection Formula from chapter 2, Key Data, we want to geek out with that person right off the bat for five minutes. You want the prospect to like you. People only buy from people they like. The sale will never happen otherwise.

This isn't something that happens by chance. You design your opening to connect with that person. And during that opening, you're *very* connected. Your conversation is not about the solution yet, it's not about the product; it's about finding something interesting in that person. When you implement this, it can't be fake or bullshit. It can't be about the weather; it can't be about something that they cannot really relate to. I have rarely ever seen a case where a sales rep cannot find *something* that they can genuinely geek out on. However, if it ever happens, then it's not the prospect for them. It should get passed to somebody else. Remember, if you're just BS-ing somebody, they will know it. You must be yourself, and your team must be themselves with every conversation.

By creating true rapport, your sales team will have increases between 25 and 35 percent, if not higher. This really does affect closing rates in a big way. Add it to your SOP.

If you really are serious about results, you want to implement this with bigger teams. Teach your team that they can't construct a version of themselves to have these conversations. It will not work.

You need to be yourself authentically. It's about bringing the power of your real experiences. The things you like, the things you don't like, the things you've experienced, the things you haven't. Ask yourself the questions "What do I like? What have I done? What have I never done? What would I like to do one day? What is important to me? What is not important to me? Where have my hobbies and my interests led me?" These are the things that you can honestly answer, because nothing is worse than getting caught in a lie in the middle of a sale. You don't want to say that you've gone on safari if you have not. It would be silly to get caught saying you've done something you haven't. Trying to connect falsely with someone in the age of social media will come back to haunt you.

In order to connect with anyone, though, you have to first understand yourself. And this applies to your reps.

Your reps must understand themselves so that they can then

connect with others. Have your team fully map this out for themselves, all of their interests and experiences. That way, they can quickly take the intelligence and apply it in the scenario before they engage in a "fight."

A great example of this is when I was selling a workshop to a prospect. LinkedIn showed that we had actually worked in the same industry at one point in our careers. So the first thing that I said when I got on the call was, "John, I see that you also worked at this company. You were my competitor. You overlapped at least one year with me." His response: "Oh my goodness, *you're* Daniel. I remember seeing you on the marketing materials for that company. Holy shit. I gotta ask you..."

Connection is a core universal strategy that *works*. In most sales organizations, this lead domino isn't properly laid. It doesn't get prioritized properly. And it derails more sales opportunities than any other single factor. You *must* make it a standard operating procedure within your organization.

ACTION STEPS

We have created a worksheet that includes a series of questions your sales team can ask themselves so that they can uncover their interests and experiences to have them first and foremost on their minds. Download at www.salesjiujitsubook.com/resources.

GO OR NO GO

GO OR NO GO: JIU-JITSU

You've connected with the opponent—either on your terms or not. Only move forward if the situation is favorable enough. Otherwise, disengage.

If your opponent pulled guard and entangled you in some form of control—it's a no go. Don't go forward. For example, if you're tied up in a spider guard, don't try to keep passing. Free yourself first, then attack on your terms.

Spider guard, an surprisingly controlling position.

Years ago, a White-Belt student was competing in his first tournament. The game plan was to win the grip battle and take his opponent down. His opponent kept grabbing his collar. Instead of deviating from the game plan, he relentlessly kept breaking the opponent's grips. The opponent would grab again; he would break again. You could see the opponent's spirit break after the eighth or ninth time. The student's relentless insistence on not engaging on the opponent's terms is what defeated his opponent, making winning the fight easy.

After sweeping my opponent in one of my first matches at the Rickson Gracie Cup mentioned above, he established a grip on my collar. No go! One grip is all you need to be able to set up a choke. I refused to take the bait and instead focused on breaking the grip and reengaging on my terms.

Connect on your terms. If it doesn't go your way, disengage and reengage in a way that suits you.

GO OR NO GO: SALES

Unless you have made human connection part of a standard operating procedure in your business, your people will not establish true rapport. If true rapport is not established, you're not going to make the sale. No matter how wonderful your product is and how perfect the solution is, if you haven't made a connection with the person you're trying to sell to, the sale will not follow. The hardest thing to master is knowing when to say no. Sometimes, though, you just have to call a spade a spade and say, "It looks like we're not able to connect. One of us must be having a hard day. I'm happy to reschedule a call or introduce you to another rep. But it's really important to me that we at least have a cordial connection. Because if we're going to go down the road of providing you a solution, I feel like we need to know each other a bit."

Sometimes even that won't work, and you need to say, "This is not going to work" and walk away. The power of that has been shown to me time and again. People will instantly change their mood because they didn't realize what they were doing and say, "Oh my goodness, I'm so sorry, I just had a fight with my wife this morning" or "My father died two weeks ago and I'm still dealing with that" or "COVID affected our business and I'm really stressed about it."

People appreciate you calling that out, because it's not okay to act like a jerk on the other side of a conversation. Eighty percent of the time that I have used that line, it turns the conversation around. Not that it always comes to a yes, but at least we establish rapport.

The other 20 percent of the time, they say something like "No, I don't feel anything's wrong; I just think this is probably a silly idea and I have better things to do." Guess what—you've just gained back an hour. If you go through the motions with someone who's not interested, you'll never get that hour back, and our time is the most precious resource we have. I would rather my team spend 80 percent of their time on the 20 percent that's going to close, rather than the opposite. When they're able to spend more of their time on prospects that have a higher chance of closing, the ones they can actually establish rapport with, sales averages go up. With more efficient use of time, you'll see your closing rates climb, along with the quality of prospects.

The better you feel, the better you perform. Nobody pays reps enough to deal with people who are completely negative.

Consider the cost. I tell my team I would rather they pick up the phone and call back a prospect with whom they had great rapport than spend more time on somebody they haven't connected with. That will lead to more sales. What won't is forcing the conversation with somebody you cannot connect with, who won't give you an inch, or who won't engage with you at all. It will certainly lead to a no.

You have to have connected with the person on something. It's pretty binary: you either got it or you didn't. If you didn't, speak up. Tell them it's not clicking. Ask for a do-over or to connect them with another rep.

Here's a motto I make my sales teams write down: "I make the commitment to myself and my time and my fellow staff and my family, and to my bank account, to bow out of situations in which I cannot get myself the massive advantage of having a connection with true rapport."

Just make a *human connection* and give yourself the opportunity to close the deal.

ACTION STEPS

Because it's not a social norm to end a conversation, have each person on your sales team write out the possible ways in which they will graciously bow out of the situation when they feel there's a no go. This way, they will have the confidence to do it when they need to. You can download some samples at www.salesjiujitsubook.com/resources.

LINE IN THE SAND

LINE IN THE SAND: JIU-JITSU

*As you start imposing your game plan, the opponent will, of course, resist. You will try to quash their resistance and you will succeed— some of the time. There will be times when their defense is successful and they are able to turn the tables so that **you** are under attack. Attacking when it's time to defend is a dangerous mistake.*

When we dream of a big win, it is often an exciting submission win— the Jiu-Jitsu checkmate. It is one of the most impressive and important aspects of Jiu-Jitsu—it actually enables you to completely disable another person, whether by "breaking them" with a joint attack or by "hitting their off switch" with a choke. It's the most dazzling part of the game by far.

In competitions, however, points are awarded for successfully estab- lishing positions so that if time runs out, there is a way to determine the winner. If you were up by points with little time left, trying to force the submission might compromise your position enough to risk the opponent earning enough points to win—or even finding a submis- sion. In a perfect world, every win would be by submission. It's the pinnacle of a match, the ultimate display of superiority. Yes, fight for submissions, but whether you get one or not, make sure to win the match. Know your line.

My first match at the 2017 No-Gi Pans was extremely close. After getting taken down, I was able to sweep my opponent with a shoulder crunch elevator sweep when he defended my armbar attempt. This tied the score. After a few attacks back and forth, it was still tied with less than a minute to go. Using one of my favorite takedowns, I was able to get him down, but not long enough to earn points. Instead, I got an advantage. The ref restarted us in the middle of the ring with only a few seconds left. Knowing I was up, I simply sat to guard, which I knew my opponent would have difficulty passing in such a short amount of time. Even though I might have liked to win with a submission or a big point difference, I knew I had done enough and elected to save my energy for the next match.

Know exactly what you need to achieve victory. You don't need a spectacular submission every time. Sometimes the smallest advantage makes all the difference. Perhaps you get an early advantage and then play conservatively. Maybe you hunt for the submission only if you have victory secured. Maybe you only attack submissions that present themselves and focus on keeping and improving your position. Knowing when you've done enough to win enables you to confidently guide the match to victory.

*Know what a win means to you. Yes, you try to make giant leaps when the opportunity presents itself, but the heart of positioning is small secure steps forward. When big openings present, of course you pounce on them, but the key in winning big is **winning**. Small wins **win**.*

LINE IN THE SAND: SALES

When I was starting my sales consulting practice, I landed one of my first meetings with a prospect. I anticipated all of the different possible scenarios. I knew he would request a percentage of my fee be paid for with his services. It would be a test, and if I were to say no to that, it would mean that I didn't believe in his services. He would ask how I could help him if I didn't believe in his services.

I also knew from other people that he was price conscious. I was high priced, but I brought high value. I said to myself, "Fifty percent is my cutoff for accepting services as payment." If he went to 55 percent, if he went to 51, that would be a hard *no*. If he was 50 or below, I would instantly say yes. I had drawn that line in the sand, and I knew where I felt comfortable engaging.

Give your team a clearly defined sandbox in which to play. The goal is to enable your sales rep to give an instant yes during a conversation and close more deals faster.

Your sales teams must know where the lines are. They know where they draw the line and where they can offer discounts, value-adds, and bonuses.

A lot of sales organizations want to keep this kind of decision close to the executive level. The problem is that when you don't disseminate the power of making these decisions to the field, to the actual sales reps who are having the conversations, it forces them to say, "Well, I've gotta check with my manager/director on that." The typical car sales scenario BS. You don't want your people to feel like car salesmen, to feel like they're in that category. They need to be autonomous within clear boundaries and be empowered to make deals happen.

That empowerment emboldens them and gives them confidence. It sends a message to the client about the rep's value. It elevates them to a higher level in the eyes of the client. That gets a higher level of mutual respect and makes sure that deal gets closed.

ACTION STEPS

Decide for yourself and your organization where you can disseminate decision-making power out to reps within the boundaries that you give them. Make it clear, with zero gray area, what happens to their commissions, what happens to their bonuses, what happens to everything—to the company, to profitability, etc. When you are transparent with your team and show them how their deals can affect areas like profitability, they will chase the most profitable deals. If you align bonuses accordingly, you are rewarding what you really want: an abundance of profitable deals.

CHAPTER 5

OPENINGS

Now that you have connected on your terms, ensured it is safe and advantageous to continue, and defined the minimum requirements for winning, how do you move forward? You start with an opening gambit—an initial attack that either works or **generates a response**. Either way, new openings emerge. You must **spot, attack**, and win them.

GENERATE A RESPONSE

GENERATE A RESPONSE: JIU-JITSU

So long as neither your go/no go benchmark nor your line in the sand has been triggered, it is safe to continue. Connecting on your terms means engaging in a way that will serve your optimal initial attacks. You must already have those attacks planned. Now, you attempt them.

Go for what you want. Either you will get it or you won't.

If you do, you have created a new, better situation. If not, whatever response you get back will create a new opportunity.

Kuzushi *is a type of "physical reverse psychology" where, knowing that the opponent will resist whatever we try, we can get them to push into us by pushing into them or get them to pull away from us by pulling away from them.*

If you do not take action, if you do not try to move forward, you give your opponent the opportunity to seize the initiative and disrupt the initial advantage you have earned. Leverage those advantages by getting them to react.

GENERATE A RESPONSE: SALES

I'll often say to my sales team, "Did you sell or were you sold?" In other words, were you taking assertive action and controlling the conversation, or was the conversation being controlled by your prospect? High-performing salespeople are good listeners. They are attuned to the art of listening to others and not to the sound of their own voices. In order to listen *and* control, you must ask the right questions. You can think of your questions as how you should break down resistance, and you use the answers to create your advantage. To get the right responses requires the right questions.

In order to ask the right questions, you must be hyper-focused on the problem that you solve for your prospect. You must be able to clearly articulate this in the language of your prospect. One of the most powerful types of questions you can ask are those that identify a specific problem that your offering can solve. What is not working in the business right now? What is broken in your systems and processes? What is the opportunity for improvement within your organization? What is a clear and present danger to your organization right now? You want to put the focus in this moment on generating a response squarely about the problem.

Don't ask a million rambling questions that have nothing to do with the problem that you solve. So many salespeople come through the school of consultative sales, thinking they are supposed to ask seventy questions, of which only ten are really relevant. Those are the ones they really want to know, but they ask all these other fluff questions that make it feel *as if* they're adding value and finding problems. All they're doing is wasting prospects' time. Clients already know their problems. You get paid to solve problems, *not* discover them.

Once you have a deep understanding of their problems and put the focus onto them, the next step is to become a specialist in solving these problems. We call it Sales Kuzushi—this is the frame that is the most powerful in any sales situation. The responses that you get will help you create a diagnosis.

If you walk into a doctor's office saying, "It hurts here on my left side," and the doctor says, "Ah, I know exactly what the problem is. Here's the left-side pill. Go home. You'll be fine in a couple of days," you are not going to trust that doctor. But if the doctor asks smart questions to really understand what you're experiencing and *then* offers a diagnosis, you'll trust the prescription.

Likewise, when you ask the right questions about the problems in a business, you set a Sales Kuzushi frame. You're able to turn around and say, "Here is how I can solve your problem with my solution." *Here's my prescription.* They will understand this for two reasons: because of the questions you ask and because your language will resonate. It will resonate because you deeply understand their problem and its impact, and can articulate it in their language.

So often we use the language of how *we* solve and view the problem and not of how *others* view the problem. Sometimes the language they use is different. We create Sales Kuzushi by asking the right questions. This allows us to spot the openings we need in order to properly devise a solution. You can't prescribe before you diagnose.

Back when I sold corporate video, I had an opportunity to pitch a company that sold candles through network marketing. At that time, video was not as prevalent as it is today. YouTube was only a year old, and businesses hadn't yet latched on to using video like they do today. We had data, however, that showed that adding a video tutorial or video marketing to a product increased sales by 18 percent.

When I met the client, I asked, "What's the biggest problem in the business right now?" They said, "We set up these micro-sites for our network marketers and they're not really converting. We spent a lot of money on custom sites for each marketer, with all of their information, picture, and all of the products, and they're just not converting. We still move product but the customers order it directly with each rep and not on the website."

So the problem was that sales were down on the site. Sales were okay in person but not on the site. I said, "Well, I've got this study, and it shows some interesting data. What if I told you that I could increase all sales on your site by 18 percent? What would that do for your business?" And all of a sudden, their faces lit up like I had given them the biggest Christmas present in the world. They said, "That'd be worth a lot of money to us."

I said, "Okay, well, it's video. And here's the study." I had it on hand. That conversation became a lucrative multiyear engagement of systematically creating sizzle videos for the different lines of candles that they placed on the site.

ACTION STEPS

Upgrade your process by using Sales Kuzushi and adding this opening question: "What is not working in the business right now?"

Develop two other opening questions that are equally powerful at revealing opportunities for your sector or niche. Figure out questions that work for your business. What opening question will instantly reveal the problems clients face?

Ensure that your teams are taking a Sales Kuzushi approach and that they're not writing a prescription or a solution before they understand the problem and they've gone through the diagnostics of that problem. If you haven't asked the right questions, don't try to write the prescription. You'll look foolish and you'll never make the sale.

SPOT THE OPENINGS

SPOT THE OPENINGS: JIU-JITSU

Compared to arts that focus on punching and kicking, Jiu-Jitsu is a soft martial art. When hitting, you're trying to quickly and fiercely invade the space the opponent occupies. By contrast, in wrestling, Jiu-Jitsu, and judo, you don't hit the person; you grab them, throw them, or pin them. You're moving into the space around them. You move into openings.

To choke someone, for example, you must move into the space around their neck.

Instead of invading the space the opponent occupies, Jiu-Jitsu teaches us to move into the space around the opponent.

Once you have attempted your opening gambit—made your initial move—you will have either moved into an existing opening or created a new one. You must learn to see openings.

After submitting my first opponent at the 2010 Abu Dhabi Pro Trials, I established strong grips in my second, aiming to pull guard. My opponent was standing upright with a hand out, ready to counter. The opportunity to pull guard wasn't really there, but he left a foot forward—I hopped in for a foot sweep. Stepping out, he caught his balance, still keeping his hand low, blocking my guard pull. Diving to the opposite side, I attacked his other leg—he used his hands to block. I attacked a foot sweep, which I knew would either work and give me the takedown or force him to step back, which he did, creating a big cavity under his chest—bingo. That cavity provided the space needed to pull guard.

By attacking the foot sweep, I generated a response—the opening necessary to take the fight where I wanted it. Seeing an opening and seizing it are not the same, but it was only because I was able to recognize the opening that I was able to take advantage of it. Learn to spot the openings your opponents leave.

Attacking the foot sweep

created the opening to pull guard. (Photo: Robert Strukelj)

SPOT THE OPENINGS: SALES

Once you've had your prospect articulate the problem in own their own language, you're going to be able to spot the openings for your solution—assuming you *fully* understand the problem. If not, keep asking clarifying questions.

Some people tend to hold back in this moment, when they spot that opening. They tend to think small instead of thinking big. When you see the opening, sometimes you need to open it even wider before you move to close the gap. You can do so by thinking really big, digging deeper into the questions, and seeing what that bigger opportunity might be. In that larger opportunity might be something that turns a $10,000 opportunity into a $25,000 opportunity. You can only do this by looking at the wider implications that digging deeper reveals.

For example, when we went in to pitch to an investment organization that worked with registered investors, they didn't have a good way of introducing the founder. They needed a way to introduce the founder's philosophy, his gravitas, his bona fides, and social proof in a powerful way. The easy answer would be a highlight reel. We found out that the founder had some image issues that the organization needed to deal with as well, and we knew the budget they had.

One of the philosophies I like to take when pitching a product or a service—especially a service-based offering—is to take a moonshot. This is an approach where you're creating three scenarios: below budget, on budget, and the moonshot. When you take a moonshot, it's the biggest, most audacious goal—with a larger budget. In my sales career, I have closed more moonshots than I can count. They capture clients' imaginations and solve their problem. Moonshots expand budgets *like nothing I've seen.* It's rare for sales reps to "take a chance" and go big. Make sure yours do.

First, we pitched the standard sizzle reel. "We'll take some news clippings, and we'll take some video from some news interviews, cutting ribbons, giving checks, putting it to some music. It would get the job done and actually come in a little under budget.

"Next would be something like that, but we'd add in some interviews that we shoot in a beautiful office and we'd interchange between the two. This would be above budget."

But then we had this other option, which was positioned like this: "Listen, my team was dreaming a little bit, and we came up with this idea, and I'll warn you now, it is a really good idea, but it is at a much bigger budget. So, I'll warn you there. We just wanted to show you how creative we could be. You may love it, you may not, but we wanted permission to tell you about it."

In our interview with the founder prior to developing the pitch, he told a story about a bricklayer. A man is walking home and sees three bricklayers laying bricks in the hot sun, all working very hard building a wall. He asks the first bricklayer, "Why are you building this wall?" He says, "It's a job. I have to do it to pay the bills and eat." Okay. Next bricklayer: "Why are you building this wall?" "I love what I do. I am a master bricklayer, and I take pride in my work." And to the last bricklayer he asks, "Why are you building this wall? Why are you working so hard?" "Ah. I'm building a house to God. I'm building the church. My community will use this church; my sons will be married here. It is for everyone that I am working this hard." He was working for a higher purpose.

The client's CEO saw himself as the third bricklayer.

The moonshot we pitched was that we'd hire a real, old bricklayer. We'd go down to a river where he would use mortar, real sand, and binder, mixing that together and actually building a wall as we told the story. You would see the weathered hands, and you'd get to see his brow beading with sweat and the old wooden wheelbarrow he used. We'd interject this with the CEO telling the story and a little bit of interview, but we'd use this as the centerpiece.

It was triple the budget. The CEO's reply to the pitch was "Done."

In that seven-year career, working in corporate video, we sold a lot of moonshots. I challenge you to find those moonshots in your business.

ACTION STEPS

Work with your team to define what a moonshot is for what you do. What are the things that go above and beyond with your product or service that would solve the client's problem so well that they would not have to be touched again for a while? How can you implement them? Is there somebody who does the training for your teams who can go out and do it one-on-one with your client? If it's a creative service, is it something that's an audacious idea?

Whatever you do, make sure you tie that to a dollar figure that supports it and ends up solving the problem so well that it becomes a profit center. I challenge you to find that in your business because when you do this for the right clients, it not only turns them into amazing fans who will get you more clients, but it will also help your team see the opportunities that they otherwise never would have. Find the moonshots in your business.

CLOSE THE GAP: JIU-JITSU

If you can't create or spot openings, you can't attack them. Equally ineffective is seeing opportunities and not attacking. If you do not attack the openings you create, you waste both energy and opportunity. You will not win that way.

How does a smaller person overcome a bigger person? There is a secret formula that all of Jiu-Jitsu is based on, developed by the Gracie family in Brazil in the 1920s. It's a three-step formula that has proven effective thousands of times over the last hundred years.

(Illustrated with photos in the Intro To BJJ section at the beginning of this book.)

Before learning it, you must understand when you are safe and when you are not. Out of range of the bigger person's punches and kicks is what Rener and Ryron Gracie, some of today's premier instructors, refer to as "the green zone"—a zone of safety. When two arms' lengths away, we are generally out of range of the opponent's attack—the "green zone". Being close enough to the opponent for them to hit you could be considered "the red zone." There is a second, secret green zone—super close to the opponent. When very close to them, you can wrap them up. They can still hit you, but not nearly as powerfully as when you are in the red zone.

Understanding this, you can keep safe by simply staying away. If they come toward you, back up. You never let them get into the red zone. The problem is that they may be faster than you, and you cannot always back up—you might hit a wall.

Step one in the three-step formula is literally called "closing the gap." If they force the red zone, we get close enough to them to tie them up in the second green zone.

Step two is to take them down to the ground—there are many ways in which to do so, depending on what openings they leave us.

Step three is to get to the mount—a completely "unfair" position for the top person. From here it is not only easy to win a fight but difficult to lose one.

In the match described earlier, I had been able to spot the opening for my guard pull, but again, seeing is never enough. You have to take action.

Pulling guard, I immediately saw another opening—the opponent's head was in front of their hips. This provides the opportunity for my favorite attack, the balloon sweep.

The balloon sweep launches the opponent overhead, normally finishing in the mount—this time, in an armbar. (Photos: Robert Strukelj)

To defend, my opponent posted his hand on the mat, providing another opening—this time for an armbar. Using the momentum of the sweep, I closed the gap he left open by wrapping my hips and legs into the space around his shoulder to secure the armbar, winning the match in about a minute.

Once you have generated responses and spotted what openings emerge, you must take action to fill them. Openings do not stay open forever. Create them. Spot them. Fill them.

CLOSE THE GAP: SALES

Solution–pain gap. Close the gap between their pain and your solution. Always remember that you get paid to solve problems!

Between your solution and their problem, or their pain, there's always a gap. Very rarely do you walk into a situation where it's a perfect 100 percent match between what you offer and what the client is looking for. There's going to be a real or perceived gap. The gap could be money. It could be that it has not been implemented in their specific niche, their business, or their industry before, but you know it could work. They've got to take a leap of faith—that's the gap.

The gap could be that there's competition. There are others that can do what you do—maybe not how you do it—but the end result is marketed as if it's the same.

Let's take CRM software, for example. They all do the same core thing, but each of them does it a bit differently—different feature benefits, different integrations, a different niche focus. Yet if you're selling it, you need to close the gap. You might be more expensive or you might be inexpensive. Each has its own way of spinning so you can close the gap.

If you have a $100,000 solution, and each piece of business is worth $25,000 to the client, then play from the power position: show them they only need to get four new clients from your solution to see a positive return on investment (ROI). The question that you need to ask is "If we solve your problem, will that help you gain at least four more clients in the next twelve months?" If the answer is yes, then it's a foregone conclusion. Just like the 18 percent increase in sales for the candle company.

Sometimes they like your solution, but they need to figure out how they're going to afford it. Make it easy for people to pay you, with simple agreements and flexible payment terms with considered multi-payment options. Other times, the issues are more nuanced.

For example, I was selling a workshop to somebody who was

trying to start their own business but was currently working for another company. He wanted our solution but could not afford it. I let him see how the main company he was working for could benefit from our solution right away. Then I said, "You could also use the knowledge and apply it to your side business." Have somebody else pay, and you go on their dime to learn and apply that learning to your own business.

I closed the gap very quickly because I had him see a connection he wasn't able to. In other cases, I helped clients to see how the product opened up a new marketplace or new opportunity that they had never thought of before. As long as I could show them where those opportunities were, they were a yes. Sometimes you have to close the gap with a little more education; other times it's simply a dollar figure. "What's your average client worth? You only need four of them to pay for our solution!" It's a foregone conclusion they will work with you. Keep in mind that ROI is a big piece.

Sometimes closing the gap means assessing on a more microscopic scale to determine where the company is with respect to the problem that they're asking you to solve. Sometimes you need to go deeper into the problem with them, using an assessment tool of some kind in order to come back with the data necessary to close the gap.

That's a situation where you need to close the gap between yourself and the more subtle insights of that situation. If you can get in there and do an hour seminar on a topic and survey them or take the executive team through an exercise, you will get the new data you need in order to close that gap. Such a tool is certainly something that you need to consider creating if you do not have something similar already.

Sometimes organizations and people want to protect themselves because maybe their department is at the heart of the problem, or maybe they're not at fault but the pain of the problem is residing in their department. Remember, they want to protect their position because it could be their job on the line if they admit that something needs fixing. The brain is designed to keep us safe. Because of that, it will let people in those positions make up excuses before they're willing to say, "Yes, there's a problem, and yes, you can help me." The brain wants to keep you safe, and by admitting there's an actual problem, it admits that there's pain: pain now and pain in solving it.

When you solve a problem, there is pain as you solve it. There's discomfort, and the brain doesn't want to let you be in discomfort. So your job is to get them to see the truth, that there is a problem, and by doing that, you have an opportunity to solve it because then you're able to close the gap and say, "This is the solution."

We're closing the gap between their understanding of their pain and their understanding of your solution's ability to solve it. Why? Because at the end of the day, that is what gets them to have an "aha!" moment. When I see that on the face of a prospect, it means they have seen the truth of the matter, and truth is the *ultimate* positioning tool. We will dive more into this in the next chapter.

My father and I decided that we were going to start a vending machine business in late 2006. My father found out that the Wrigley organization had purchased $1.5 million worth of vending machines that didn't work, and he saw a problem that he might be able to solve. The pain they felt was having machines that needed to be in the marketplace selling gum but could not because they didn't work. Furthermore, the person who green-lighted the project had his job at risk.

My father came to me and said, "You're smart. How can we make these things work?" After some research and finding the right partners, we were able to figure out how to retrofit the machines so they worked. We approached Wrigley and said, "We can make the pain go away. Give us all the machines for a dollar, and we will not only make them work, but we'll retrofit them all. We'll sell them as vending machine businesses for people to operate. That will do a few things. They'll buy your gum to fill the machines. The machines will go into places where gum is not normally sold, people will get the gum, you will earn more market share, and you'll get a $1.5 million write-off this year because we will take them off your hands. You'll make an impact. You'll take the write-off. We'll make it happen for you."

They said yes because we closed the gap for them; we came in and directly solved the problem and understood how to secure that position with them. There was zero risk for them. We made it into a zero-risk scenario. We demonstrated that the machines worked, and we created the entire business model in order to solve that problem. Then we sold over twenty-five thousand machines across Canada within a year.

ACTION STEPS

Explore with your team and brainstorm to create diagnostic tools in the form of assessments or interviews so you can say, "Okay, we're going to do this analysis. It takes thirty minutes, and it's with your executive team. At the end of the analysis, we'll be in a position to recommend the proper solution to your problem, and we'll give you the results of the analysis in a report, just for giving us the time."

Remember that they can't do much with this; ultimately, it's not you *implementing* the solution you're recommending, so giving them value in exchange for their time is the price you pay for stepping onto the mat. The alternative is a weak position and not getting a solid chance to win.

CHAPTER 6

POSITIONING

Positioning is the heart of Jiu-Jitsu, the core principle on which all of it is based. It is the highest form of leverage. From a good position, things are easy. From a bad position, things are hard. Don't try to win the fight from where you are. Position yourself so that winning is inevitable. You do this first by **securing any position** you earn. Then you must **improve your position** with the ultimate goal of **setting up your win**.

SECURE YOUR POSITION

SECURE YOUR POSITION: JIU-JITSU

Once you have closed the gap between yourself and the opportunities you have created, dig your heels in. **Keep** *your position. You have invested too much time and energy into this fight to let the advantages you have earned slip away.*

*A common mistake one sees when watching White Belts (novices) compete is that as soon as they get to a good position, they immediately try to jump to the next good position. For example, if the top person passes the guard—gets around the legs of the bottom person and into side control—they'll immediately try to mount the opponent rather than taking the time to (a) really secure the position they have earned or (b) make sure the path is clear to move forward. In making this mistake, not only do they not go forward one step into mount, but they are often put **back** a step or two, stuck in the opponent's guard.*

In the 2010 Ontario Open, I was fighting from my guard and used a combination attack. Sliding my hand deep inside the opponent's collar, I threatened a choke. Defending by placing his hand on my bicep to keep my free hand away, he left himself open to an armbar, which I rotated under him to attack. As he defended, I was able to flip him over and get on top, but as I did, his arm had slipped enough that he was able to destabilize my position. I could have kept fighting for the armbar, but this would have jeopardized my ability to stay on top. Instead, I grabbed his head and pulled my way into the mount, not only securing my two points for the sweep, but another four for the mount.

Your first job, once you've established a new position, is to secure it and make sure you don't lose an inch of ground in the wrong direction.

SECURE YOUR POSITION: SALES

Once you've identified how to close the gap, it's the moment of truth, because you've seen how you can close the solution to the pain-point gap. *Now* is the time to secure that position with your prospect.

So often your position is defined by the truth of the situation. You're seeking the raw truth that is sometimes buried for your prospect one to three levels deep. Putting a spotlight on the truth is ultimately going to secure your position.

With the success of the Canadian experience with Wrigley's, the US side wanted in. However, the reason it was so successful in Canada was that the currency has one-dollar and two-dollar coins, and coin mechanisms are cheap, efficient, and don't break down. American consumers don't use dollar coins. But Wrigley still wanted us to solve the problem in the United States.

How do we translate the Canadian experience of the success of these machines into the United States? I went through figuring out how to make it happen. The problem that I had to solve was the dollar bill. This was before we had credit-card tapping or contactless card readers. America was still very much a cash society and dollar bills were the major form, so we'd have to transact with paper currency.

The problem was figuring out how to create a machine that could do that in a way that was efficient and easy and could be put up anywhere. I went and researched in China for what exists on the market that can do this. The answer lay in now-unused cigarette machines. With a little bit of digging and some translation software, I was able to read the Chinese sites, approached an organization, and asked them to do a retrofit on a current cigarette machine.

I sent them the gum and said, "Make your cigarette machines push this out instead." By sending $3,000 to China, we acquired an elegant solution that took one-dollar bills, was battery-driven, required no plug, and was a wall-mounted machine.

We had the solution. It was very elegant, but what would stop a multinational organization from simply copying it once we gave them the idea? Instead of going through the thousands and thousands of dollars and months if not longer to copyright the IP, we positioned ourselves so winning would be easy. We told Wrigley, "We've come up with a solution. We've tested it, and it works. This isn't blowing smoke up your butt. Our only condition in sharing the solution is you have to sign this simple nondisclosure, noncompete."

They stalled. They stalled for many days, and I think they were trying to figure it out. Then we got our call from our main contact, Frank, which was the make-or-break call, and I said, "We're not going to have this conversation until you sign the document." He replied, "Well, a lot of people say that they've come up with something unique. I want to list out all the things that I've thought of first before I sign." He listed tokens and money exchangers that took the bill and gave you a token, or the business owner would provide the token and the person had to go there to give the money and get a token, or it only took quarters. He came up with all these other solutions that I discounted because they're too clunky. I said, "It's none of those. I can guarantee you; it is not any one of those." He said, "Okay. I'll sign the document," because now he was super curious. He wanted to know because he had invested all that time and energy.

We got the document signed, held the meeting, and we blew his mind. *Absolutely* blew his mind. He didn't think something like this was possible. Eight months later, we had a seventy-five-page, highly detailed negotiated contract, but the main positioning tool to get there was protecting the intellectual property.

Remember, if they don't agree that they have a problem, you won't be able to see their pain point and you'll never secure a good position with them. You must determine if you're going to spend more time or walk away from this prospect.

ACTION STEPS

Sometimes in order to get or provide information, you need to sign nondisclosure agreements. Or you might need to have one signed. Either way, just do it. The more I signed in my twenty-five years of sales, the more sales I made. Nothing gets to the truth faster than a legal document that keeps secrets.

IMPROVE YOUR POSITION

IMPROVE YOUR POSITION: JIU-JITSU

It is true that you can submit someone from a dominant position, and so it would make sense to try to submit them if you have attained a dominant position. However, each good position is better than the last. Each next, better position offers even more control and submission opportunity than the last. Even within the same position there are better and worse variations.

For example, there are many variations of the mount, from "low" to "high." Generally, the lower versions offer more control, and the higher versions offer more submission opportunity.

In the fight described earlier, where I let go of the armbar to secure the mount, I spent nearly forty seconds in a low mount, shutting down the opponent's escapes before eventually sliding to a mid-mount, from which I could sit up and start attacking the opponent's collar to threaten a choke.

Make small, secure improvements consistently.

IMPROVE YOUR POSITION: SALES

In order to keep improving your position, you need to maintain control of the conversation. It's very easy for the conversation to get away from you even after you've shown them that you can solve their problem. Why does this happen? For a couple of reasons. It comes back to the brain wanting to keep us safe; admitting that there is a problem and thinking about the process of solving it can be painful. It could bring up vulnerabilities, making a prospect's brain come up with excuses just to keep them safe. Safe in their career, safe with shareholders or the board of directors. These things are worries.

Some people will never show weakness by admitting there's a problem in the first place. Sometimes that is where the initial pushback comes. At this point in the conversation, what I normally like to do is recap where we are in the conversation. Using their words to describe the problem allows you to frame the solution.

The key to improving your position is to ensure that you don't lose control of the conversation. This is normally where they're asking questions. It can very easily spiral out of your control. The questions they ask will tend to bring up objections, which we're going to talk about in the next chapter. It may bring the fight-or-flight response, as they realize that the problem is bigger than them. It's amazing how many excuses they will come up with as to why it's okay to just "leave it alone."

At this point when you've made it so clear what the problem is, the ramifications of that problem not being solved may cross to other domains within the organization. You need to check for what I call *hidden decision makers*, because ultimately in today's organizations, it's not one person making a decision. Most decisions are made as a group.

With most sales conversations at this point, you need to check in and say, "Now that we understand what the problem is, who are the people in the organization who need to be in a position to sign off and might raise concerns about solving this problem?" You haven't even touched presenting your solution yet. Who has to be around the table to solve this, to be approving a project from all angles of the problem?

Then they say, "Oh, right. We probably should bring finance in" or "Yeah, you're right. We need to bring operations, maybe marketing. I might want to have a couple of sales guys there." You can secure your position with that individual, but they are not always the ultimate decision maker. You need to check in at this point in order to improve your chances of having the right people around the table so that when you do present your solution, it's presented to the right brains in the organization, who will be able to say yes.

I was once selling corporate video to an insurance company. The director of marketing is a great guy. We had a couple of really good meetings dialing down to understanding what was going on with their prospects and what kind of video tools could move the needle for them to increase their sales. What kind of tools would resonate with the different niches that they were going after, and how could we create some tools that would really speak to those people? We were talking about ethnic niches, which can be a sensitive topic.

The conversation was going great, and that's when I asked him, "Now that we're talking about corporate strategy, niche strategy, we're talking about representing the brand—shaping the brand around the different niches, being able to really speak their language. Who else in the organization should be signing off on this kind of project—not only the size of project that we're talking about now, because the scope has gotten pretty big from a dollars perspective—but also who needs to read into this to ultimately say yes?"

He sat back and said, "Shit. Yeah. We probably need the whole leadership team, because any one of them could raise concerns, and I can't represent what you have come up with. You guys have to come and present that."

"Cool. Give me the names, who they are, LinkedIn profiles. Give me what their titles are, what their responsibilities are. Give me a little bit of information about how long they've been with the organization, maybe something they did just before this role."

He got the information to us, and we were able to think through our presentation in order to maximize the results in the room by understanding and thinking, "Well, this person is going to have comments from this angle. They're going to have these concerns. This person is in this position now but was in this other position before, and so we should expect these kinds of objections." The key point here is our contact couldn't represent the pitch like we could. If we didn't take this step and we simply did the pitch to him, there probably would have been a 50 percent chance of the deal not happening.

What I would recommend is first making sure you have that champion excited, understanding the problem, and feeling like you are the right fit. Then bring in all the decision makers. What salespeople sometimes do is ask for all the decision makers too soon, before they have really secured their position. They do it all the way at the top of the process before they understand the problem fully or have been able to figure out how to close the gap. They haven't figured out a lot of the key elements; it's too soon and the opportunity doesn't go anywhere. This happens when reps don't get to the place of ultimate clarity. Once you have that clarity by working with your champion, *then* ask for the hidden decision makers to join you around a table. That way, you frame the conversation and win the deal!

ACTION STEPS

Review your recent sales wins and create a profile of your ideal champions. You might need to break these into niche or industry. Check if your champion was the ultimate decision maker or if there were hidden decision makers as well. If so, who were they and what were their positions? Determine the optimal time in your sales process to bring up the hidden decision maker. How can you apply this to your current sales engagements?

SET UP YOUR WIN

SET UP YOUR WIN: JIU-JITSU

Once we have secured our position and improved it, where do we go? To victory, of course—the submission. In a sense, however, a submission is just another position. Just as we want to be careful to secure our positions, we want to treat submission with the same care.

When you attack your opponent's neck with a choke, predictably their hands will come up to protect it. That separates their elbows from their body, creating a little bit of space in their armpits.

When I was threatening the choke from the mount in the fight described in the previous chapter, the opponent defended with his hands. I could have jumped for the armbar directly, but instead, I slid up to a high mount—again, the higher up the opponent's body, the more control you have. After securing my position when I first got to the mount, I improved my position by sliding high.

From there, the choke is an even greater threat, creating what famed Jiu-Jitsu instructor John Danaher calls "dilemmas"—circumstances with few options, all of which lead to bad outcomes for the opponent. Under still greater threat of choke, the opponent bucked and pushed wildly, allowing me to climb higher still to S-mount, where the armbar is imminent.

Every (classic) armbar requires our hips to be glued to the opponent's armpit. If our hips are far from their armpit, we won't be able to finish.

Hips far—notice how low the arm can go without causing the opponent to tap.

Hips tight—notice how much sooner the submission comes on.

You have secured a good position and improved it into an even better one. Victory is in sight. It's almost time to seal the deal. Instead of going in for the kill now, go the extra mile and **make sure** *you win. Improve your position so much that when it is time to claim victory, the outcome is inevitable.*

SET UP YOUR WIN: SALES

To ensure that you have the right people in the room, start by recapping the understanding of the problem using the language the prospect already agreed to from Generating a Response. Once you have done the recap, ask them to think about what will happen if they don't solve the problem. This is going to serve you well at the end of the conversation when you hook them with the cost of inaction. Be aware that there is a big difference between when this is something *they* tell *you* and when you tell it to them. In other words, if somebody owns the statement of consequences, it should be the prospective client and not you. Psychologically, when they can articulate what could happen if they do not solve this problem, they own the statement. You are then better able to layer the conversation and hit them with the cost of inaction (COI) later on. The COI is what will happen if they do not solve the problem. It is a cost factor.

You're better able to frame the problem through their lens if the client does not resist this point later on. You can't deal with that resistance at the end when you're trying to close. You need to set up the COI now to deal with any of that resistance prior to presenting the solution.

If you reverse it and you start to talk about the cost of inaction before you present the solution, it will feel as if you're manipulating them. Rather, we want them to own the COI. You simply bring it out later in the conversation, through an ROI lens, which we'll talk about in the next chapter. You're thinking six moves ahead, knowing that you're going to need this as a closing tool.

I was selling a high-end telecom product that was a great maximizer of print campaigns. It was a short code system where, from any cell phone, you could hit pound and a three- or four-digit code to instantly connect you with the company's 800 number.

We came up with four-digit combinations that spelled out a word that was on-brand for a travel organization. We knew through an outdoor display company contact that they had just purchased a very large order of marketing display spots. They purchased an advertising window, a very aggressive one. We knew that with the short code they not only could measure how many people were using the code, they also would increase the amount of activity coming from those print ads an average of 15 to 20 percent, which is what our data was showing.

When we went in to talk to them, we asked them what their tracking strategy was and what their conversion rates were from the print ads. I asked what it would be worth to them if they were able to track conversions. They said, "We don't really know—we've never had a way to track results."

I said, "If you were able to track the performance of the print campaign, you could make a decision in the future whether or not to do it in the first place. What if I told you we could not only help you get 15 to 20 percent more out of future ads, but help you even get that value out of the money you already invested in that outdoor campaign?

Through discussion, they agreed these were the problems they faced. They saw that by adding our solution to their campaign, they were going to be able to track response, so now they could determine the ROI of their marketing activity. Then I asked, "What will that mean to you?"

Their response: "Well, we can hire more staff. We could maybe open up another store if it goes well."

It was a foregone conclusion that they wanted it. The win was set up.

This is how you ensure that the organization understands that they should fix this now and not later. It's a bit of a dance at this point. Sometimes they won't own it. Sometimes they just will push back; and, yes, sometimes the deal still doesn't happen.

It's got to be sticky. It's got to be them owning that COI, not you. If they do, your win is set up.

ACTION STEPS

Figure out the best framing of the problem you're solving as it relates to the solution you're about to provide for your next sale. Understand the questions you need to ask in order to get the answers that you need to win the sale. Once you have established this, create a system so you can figure this out for every sale moving forward.

PART III

WINNING

Most people fail in their endeavors because they're not as careful in the end as they are in the beginning.

—*TAO TE CHING*

It's easy to think of a submission as one technique, but it's a process. Just as we want to master the process of getting here, we want to master the process of securing victory. This is why we're here.

We begin by attacking the **submission**, then look to **reinforce** it before finally **finishing** it. We have done the work to create, increase, and seize openings. It's time to finish the fight.

CHAPTER 7

SUBMIT—FINISH THE FIGHT

This is what it's all about—submission. Ultimate victory.

Again, it's not a single act, it's a process.

First you **attack** your finishing move. Then you **reinforce** the advantage gained. Then you pull the trigger—execute the **finish**.

ATTACK THE SUBMISSION

ATTACK THE SUBMISSION: JIU-JITSU

The fight will not finish itself. Once you have done all this work and created this opportunity, you must seize it. The opening won't be there forever. To do the work to get here and to not pull the trigger is just as ineffective as never getting here.

In the fight mentioned in the previous chapter, I had climbed high in the mount all the way to S-mount. Sensing the danger, the opponent started bucking wildly, trying to press me off with his arms. This destabilized my position but left his arm open for a split second. I pounced on it.

The armbar can be set up slowly or pounced on.

Sometimes attacking the submission means diligently setting it up and moving into it steadily, and sometimes it means catching the opportunity as it's presented. The window of opportunity may only open for a brief moment. Being able to catch submissions as they present themselves is a matter of preparation, timing, and decisiveness.

Yes, we want to slowly and steadily improve our positions, but when opportunities appear, we must be able to seize them.

ATTACK THE SUBMISSION: SALES

The job of the elite sales rep is to go for the close. Now you have everything you need in order to effectively present the solution. One of the first things I say is "I'm 100 percent confident I can help you solve all the problems that we've talked about." And then I'll explain why: "Since we've worked with many organizations like yourself and had XYZ success" or "Here is the success record we've had in the marketplace" or "This solution has been proven because of these implementations" or "The product is going to perform because..." or "It's going to outperform for you because..." and describe what they said.

Present the solution as the solution to all of the problems *you spoke about*. Don't widen the scope beyond what was discussed. This will cause interference in the mind of your prospect. It's one of the biggest mistakes I see. If you bring up another benefit that you did not already talk about, it makes the brain think too hard. At this point, you want nodding heads and agreement. What you don't want is confusion or the prospect stopping you for clarification because you forgot to mention something during your last meeting. If there are aspects to the solution that you know might add value, *don't talk about it now*. Doing so will actually be counterproductive at this point. Now is the time to make sure that you're super clear on the scope and actually freaking nail it for them in their heads.

As you move into a high-level conceptual overview of how you're going to solve the problem, you don't want to present a step-by-step instruction manual. You don't even want to give them the big picture of the solution. You want to tell them how the solution will solve their problem and what the major steps are that you will be taking in order to solve it.

So many people go into "I need to look like a genius" mode and actually solve the problem in the moment, which is a disservice. They don't have everything they need to solve it fully anyway. They have a lot of information, but they don't know how to *implement* it. Some organizations will take that little bit of information and try to implement it and ultimately fail, and they probably won't come back to you. They'll probably find another vendor, so be careful.

Ultimately, if you feel that you can solve the problem for them, you owe it to them to make sure that you are giving them just enough information so that they can say yes, but not too much information so that they feel like they can go do it themselves.

In the process of presenting the solution, as you come to the conclusion of it, you're simply asking them, "Can we solve this for you? Can we partner with you to solve this problem and solve it for good, once and for all?"

I was selling a sponsorship opportunity at a major financial conference. There were five hundred top-end bankers, each spending over $2,000 to attend a three-day conference in Whistler, British Columbia. The event brought together global players in asset-backed securities. (This was before the 2008 recession.) A European bank was a new player in the market, and they really wanted to make a big impact and meet a lot of people at this event so they could leave with some deals made. That was the problem they needed to solve: how to get the maximum amount of people interested in meeting with them so they could ink some deals.

All of the top sponsorship positions were already filled, so I came up with a new opportunity that specifically solved their problem.

The solution I came up with was to have the room keys for all attendees custom-printed. Each key was a business card for the main contact of the European bank who was there, the top person who was coming to the event. Now every attendee had that card as their room key, and the European bank couldn't have been happier with the results. I presented a solution that addressed the specific problem they were trying to solve.

It molded directly to the opening that was presented to me. That opportunity brought in the same amount of money as a top-level $100,000 sponsorship because there was so much value behind it.

ACTION STEPS

It's imperative that your sales team understands the best possible way to position themselves. How do they present a solution so well tailored that it becomes a no-brainer, so that the client simply must go with your solution? Prepare those scenarios during a brainstorming session.

Also think about your current prospects and where you're not presenting the strongest solution in a direct way. How can you turn it around so that your client understands that your solution will solve the problem 100 percent?

REINFORCE THE SUBMISSION: JIU-JITSU

Attacking the submission and getting the tap don't always happen simultaneously. A submission is its own position and it still serves you to continue to improve that position by increasing your degree of control.

Making small adjustments that increase control of the arm or neck is positioning applied to the armlock or choke. When attacking the armbar, for example, one of the first instructions we are taught is to squeeze our knees together. This pinches the opponent's arm with our thighs, greatly limiting their movement while decreasing the effort needed to complete the submission (not to mention protecting one's groin!). By trapping their wrist with our elbow, we glue their arm to us and control their wrist, again making escape difficult.

Both arms control the opponent's, making it tough to get out.

When attacking from the back in the gi, you can finish the person with a two-collar choke. Sometimes when you can't get the necessary grip because it is out of reach or you are blocked by the opponent, you can attack the "bow and arrow" choke. To **secure** *the choke, you must lock your legs over the opponent's shoulders and grab their pants at the knee. Once here, you are in excellent finishing position. As the grip on the knee can be broken, you can further reinforce the choke by hugging the opponent's leg—a* **very** *difficult grip to break. If you are particularly flexible, you can reinforce further by stepping your foot over the opponent's shoulder and crossing your ankles. This increases your leverage, enabling you to finish.*

The bow and arrow choke

Reinforcement is important not only for increasing control and security, but because, as we'll see in the next chapter, we are likely to face resistance in multiple forms. And whereas joint locks are binary— they either do take the joint past its natural range of motion or they don't—chokes require time to finish. Reinforcement hinders escape attempts and provides the added control needed to have time for the choke to take effect.

REINFORCE THE SUBMISSION: SALES

Once you've had a solid presentation of your solution, it's time to reinforce the client's belief in both you and the solution by painting a picture of the solution actually being implemented: *future casting*. What does the future of their company look like using your solution? What are the positive repercussions of implementing your solution? These can be short-term, medium-term, or long-term results. In the European bank example, it was an instant result. On the first day of the conference, they had opportunities to connect. It could be an increase in sales, it could be an increase of customer service, which could ultimately lead to more sales, customer or employee retention, etc. It could be a recruitment tool for HR to find better talent, which will increase the company's overall positioning. It could be a training tool that shapes culture at an organization. The most important thing is to not deviate from what you just presented, as it will leave the brain confused, and confused prospects don't buy.

This is a step that a lot of organizations miss. They miss *future casting* the vision of what life will be like a year from now, after they've said yes. It's like envisioning what their yes will mean to them and to the company. And if you can get your decision maker to see themselves as a hero, that will only help your positioning.

This is why you need to ask great questions: you need to know the answers to what is most important to them and the organization. Having your prospect give this to you allows you to embed it throughout the close.

I was working with an international engineering firm that had a product that could survive in a fire for two hours. It's used in major hospitals, police stations, bridges, government buildings, etc., to allow critical systems to keep working during a fire. The problem was that the product was expensive and hard to install, so they had two issues: how to market a more expensive solution and how to have it be perceived as being straightforward to install. The first solution was a great marketing video; the second took more digging. I asked how they get over the objections around the complicated install. They include the cost to fly out their master installers to work with local contractors, helping them map out the install and be with them to troubleshoot. It cost them $100,000 annually in travel expenses alone.

I proposed creating an extremely detailed video walkthrough that had *every* small detail on it that the installers could load on an iPad and take to a site. It would be so detailed that the firm could stop sending out staff members. I asked, "Would that be valuable to you?" They said, "Hell, yes!" and paid $100,000 to save that and the staff's time the following years. It became a great tool to help them sell more of the wiring.

I worked with an organization that ran retirement homes. They had a problem with their meal service staff: they were not running the dining rooms at a consistent level of service across all of their high-end retirement homes. Dinners are supposed to be served as if it were a five-star hotel. It's all plated service, everything from the way the cutlery is laid out to how the wine is offered, how the plates are put down, the timing, the I, the expectation of how the guests dress. Everything is at a high level, but there was a consistency issue and they needed training tools that would help streamline the entire organization.

The first solution they tried was to send out training teams. But that's costly, and how do you deal with new staff? It's expensive to fly people out to do days of training yearly. The solution we came up with was a series of video curricula. Everybody in the organization, from the frontline staff to the managers, would have to go through a learning-management software system that tracked their progress and issued a certificate.

So, for them, I said, "Well, imagine a year from now that every single staff member, from day one of coming onboard, has the exact same training, knows the exact same standards. Then in the future if something goes wrong, a manager can have them redo that part of the training as a reinforcer. What would happen in your organization, if that level of consistency was obtained by all your frontline serving staff?"

Their answer was "Amazing things."

Ultimately, this was more of a long-term play for customer retention. The cost of high-end retirement homes is so significant, retention is a big deal.

Another example was working with a medical laboratory services company who found out that a lot of their patients were coming in unprepared for particular diagnostic tests, imaging tests, and even getting blood taken. This was confusing and delayed delivering their services. They served a diverse population of people who spoke English as a second language. They didn't have an efficient way to communicate how to prepare for tests to that population. And, facing stiff competition, they were also seeking to get more market share.

Our solution was to create a series of informational videos that we translated into multiple languages. The videos would explain each procedure in a universal way and make it feel less scary for the patient. They would ensure that the patient felt prepared. Then there would be an outreach program to doctors to advise that patients watch these before they booked appointments. They loved it.

To reinforce the solution, I *future-cast* by asking, "What do you think your organization's uptick in people choosing you over your competitor will be when your patients have had these resources at hand? What will it be like when they show up for tests with this level of preparation? What will it be like when it becomes known within newcomer communities that you have resources that are translated into multiple languages?"

They saw a really good vision of the future with this solution, and we won the deal.

ACTION STEPS

Make sure to add *future casting* to your SOP and pick your next top-five active prospects right now. Paint the picture of what each of their companies is going to be like with your solution deployed by creating a one-pager for each. Often in sales the best storyteller wins!

FINISH THE SUBMISSION

FINISH THE SUBMISSION: JIU-JITSU

Once we have locked in the submission, it's time to pull the trigger. Attacking an arm, a leg, or the neck with a choke means going from a position of control—guard, side control, mount, or the back—to a "sub-position"—a position in which you somehow coil yourself around the arm, leg, or neck of the opponent in such a way that you can disable or choke them.

In one possible game plan, you engage, create an opening, take them down, pass their guard, mount them, secure the mount, and slide up to a high mount and eventually an S-mount. From there you:

- *Attack the submission—throw your leg over the opponent's head to position yourself to armlock the opponent*
- *Secure the submission—pinch your knees together, wrap their wrist with your elbow, hand grabbing your trap*
- *Finish the submission—lie back and, if necessary, lift your hips. In training and competition, the opponent taps because that move has the potential to do some serious, painful damage to the arm. A submission will put the opponent to sleep or cause them to have a body part seriously dislocated, torn, or broken if they do not tap.*

This is the final step. It's time to seize victory—to finish the match.

FINISH THE SUBMISSION: SALES

This is the point when pricing is formally presented. Now that you understand your exact solution and the scope of it, you can get granular. (This assumes that you have qualified your prospect before entering into the sales process in the first place. If you are not able to fully qualify your prospect, then before ending your first meeting, make sure to mention what budgets typically support your kind of solution. This will open the door to talk about what budget ranges they typically spend to solve these kinds of problems.)

There are two schools of thought on the formal presentation of pricing. The first one is *the price is the price*. There are no discounts on the price. It is the value of your service for your product, and you reinforce this value again here.

Other people feel that they need to build up the value of the product and say, "Here is what we're prepared to offer you: a discount, a value-add, incentives, etc.," which we'll get into in the next chapter. My personal preference is that the price is the price, and if you've done your job well to this point, you've built the value of working with you, the real value of solving their problem. In other words, once you solve their problem, how long before they see some ROI. This is really easy when you're dealing with a product or service that brings in more sales.

You ask, "Each client is worth how many dollars?" Then you take what those dollars are, and you divide by your price. And now they need five more clients, ten more clients, one hundred more clients—whatever the number is to reinforce the investment in your product or service.

The challenge is that it's not always a direct money-generating or revenue-generating return. Sometimes you have to value it against increased productivity or preventing a loss of profits. Your pitch may be around preventing a loss of clients, staff retention, increased market share, etc. Now these things could themselves eventually be tied back to profits and to the acquisition of new clients, but there's not a direct correlation, not a direct A to B line. Find the opportunity to present the value of the pricing so that it justifies the investment in the mind of your prospects.

At Advance Your Reach, we help individuals, entrepreneurs, and organizations leverage speaking on digital and physical stages as a major client acquisition source. We provide "done with you" workshops that are sold at events, webinars, and one-on-one video calls. Typical investments are between $10,000 and $25,000. One of the early questions we ask in the sales process is "How much is your average client worth to you?" By understanding that, we are able to say, "Well, when you're on your first stage, giving your amazing talk, do you think you can land (then I say a number that makes sense based on those investments) perhaps two or three clients? Then you have 100 percent ROI on your first stage."

And 95 percent of them say, "I can do that." Making the investment becomes a no-brainer. This only happens if you've already done a really good job presenting the solution, understanding what it's going to be like for them to serve those new clients and what problem it solves for them. The price has to be in line with the value you bring to the organization. You need to find the ROI that's there, and when you're presenting the price, it must be through that lens of the value it brings to the organization.

ACTION STEPS

Figure out your perfect formula that demonstrates your ROI. In the case of the workshop company, it's simply how many clients equals how many dollars. In other cases, the formula is going to be more complicated. Determine if there is a universal formula that you can apply to every sales deal or if you need to custom-create one for each new deal.

CHAPTER 8

COUNTERS

As we look to seal the deal, our opponent will inevitably look for a countermove, commonly referred to simply as a counter, to turn the tables. There will always be last-minute resistance. We must be diligent in preparing for and **preventing** it. If they are able to actually mount a counter, we must be ready to **counter** that counter and **break** their resistance in order to guarantee our emerging successful on the other side. This is just one more layer between us and ultimate victory. We must prepare for it.

PREVENT ESCAPES

PREVENT ESCAPES: JIU-JITSU

Every move has a counter. Every submission can be stopped and escaped from. Yes, we want to be able to recounter and stop someone once they've started to counter, but far superior is to prevent them from escaping in the first place. This is your pre-fight work—intelligence and strategy. Knowing what to do, when.

Now it's time to act on what you know, not only securing the submission but preventing escapes. Ideally, you planted the seeds of immobility before you even attacked the submission, but once you get here, there is more work to do. Make escape impossible.

When you go for an armbar, for example, your opponent can use the "hitchhiker escape"—turn their thumb down toward their ear while walking away to their knees. By turning their thumb in the opposite direction in advance, we make the hitchhiker impossible.

A great example of preventing the escape was used in a famous match between two BJJ legends, Eddie Bravo and Royler Gracie. Eddie had developed his own way of controlling from the guard that seemed incredibly effective, and he was talking big game about how he was going to win the tournament. Royler had never been tapped in tournament in his weight class and was able to pass Eddie's guard a number of times. Eddie was able to get out with some of his own unique techniques and wrap Royler up—and after threatening a sweep, which Royler defended, Eddie caught him in a triangle choke.

One of the primary escapes for the triangle is to step over the opponent's head, lie back, and cross your ankles to pry their legs open.

The triangle choke can be escaped from if we can step over the opponent's head.

*The typical way of grabbing that leg, is to reach underneath it. Instead, Eddie deftly wrapped **over** it, trapping it, making it impossible for Royler to use that extremely strong escape.*

Wrapping **over** the leg, Eddie was able to prevent the step-over escape and finish the choke.

Anyone can hit a triangle, but to hit one on a legend like Royler was a testament to the power of Eddie's innovations. But at the same time, to counter his escape before it even happened—that was, to me, the impressive part and the real key to victory in that match, which cemented his name in the Jiu-Jitsu history books.

You have come this far. Tie up all loose ends. Don't leave success to chance.

PREVENT ESCAPES: SALES

Long before you get into presenting the solution, you have to be seeding the objection-busting stories and points. In other words, take a look at the objections database that you've created and bake objection prevention both into your marketing *and* into your solution. Into the stories of our implementation, stories of results people have gotten, of people using our products and how we delivered outstanding service. Bake them into the features and benefits. Bake them in so much that, essentially, there are no longer any objections. There's nothing prospects can say that you haven't already addressed. And even if they do, you can say, "Well, listen, that's a great question/concern that we get all the time." Then direct them back to one of the stories you have already told.

Sometimes, however, you will have to completely deal with this objection.

I always liked to think of objection handling as something that you answer with a story, with an anecdote. They're much more powerful than simply saying, "Oh, yeah, well, we handle that through this feature or this benefit." It's more powerful to say, "Oh, well, that reminds me of the time that we worked with the

ABC company, and they had the same issue. They implemented our solution, and this was the result. And because of that result, they've been able to do XYZ. We see this issue time and again within your industry; that is why it shouldn't be a concern for you."

You want to get to a place where you're so effective at proactively handling objections that during this point in the process it's only new ones that catch you off guard. Then you are super diligent about getting them logged into your objections database and working them into your training in the days and weeks to come. The goal of the elite sales team is to get to a point where you're so good at this that there isn't anything new that comes your way; you have already baked all objections into the different areas of your marketing or your pre-sale process.

When I first started working with the corporate video company I've mentioned, we did not have video in our own marketing. We did not have any of the video tools we were suggesting to clients to leverage as an organization to sell our services. That was a big hole in the value proposition. You can't sell something that you're not using yourself.

We started to systematically create testimonial videos that were linked to common objections that we got within the sales process. The big one that comes up for everybody, and I don't care what industry you're in, is about price. So, we addressed that directly with some champion clients using a series of video clips of them talking about the price they paid and the value that they got. Other topics were quality and the creative process. The videos worked great and allowed me to double sales that year. This proved to me that it's better to have your clients answering objections for you with a tool like a video testimonial than to tell them about a client yourself.

When clients can answer for you on your behalf, it's a much better power position than you telling a story. Having the prospect hear from a client can be a very effective countermove. I once worked with a car dealership that wanted to sell service packages as an add-on. We created a video series that addressed the value that other clients got from the service packages and made sure they were from different ethnic backgrounds, based on their demographics and geographical area.

The car sales rep would say, "You know what, I'm going to check with my manager about financing. While I'm gone, I'll just throw this video on. It kind of speaks to some of the stuff we were talking about and gives the perspective of a couple of other clients who had a chance to sit down with us and talk a little bit about their experience. I'm sure you guys will get some great benefits. I'll be back in about three minutes." They would play the video, walk out of the room, then come back. Now prospects had the perspective of people who had benefited in the exact areas where they had concerns. It was an extremely effective way of countering objections when they did come up.

At any time in the sales process, you can use a video to help prevent or overcome objections.

ACTION STEPS

Ensure that your objections database is being utilized and establish protocols around this. Audit your current customers, asking them why they decided to work with you, and then develop the resources that will proactively bust objections using the answers you hear.

COUNTER ESCAPES

COUNTER ESCAPES: JIU-JITSU

However diligent you are in security and prevention, you will seek to contend with better and better opponents. Eventually, you will meet some who is able to foil your checkmate, escape your submissions. While some opponents may have tapped by this point, some will continue to work to get out.

Persistence is vital—we must follow through, but the real work here should have been done when game-planning: studying the ins and outs of how people might try to escape when we are about to win. This is the endgame. We have to continue to chase. If they move away, we follow. Studying the ins and outs of this part of the game is the homework we had to do when game-planning. If they try to escape, we must stay the course and not allow them to change positions or reset to a safe spot. Once we have victory in our sights, we have to seize it.

In the finals of the 2010 Ontario Open, I attacked a guillotine choke from my guard. The opponent tried to counter by pulling down on my choking wrist. Noticing his defending elbow too close to his ribs, I jumped my legs over his arm to recounter with a triangle choke, which won me the match.

*In the epic battle between Marcelo Garcia and Kron Gracie, Marcelo— after escaping a few guillotine chokes himself—caught **Kron** in a guillotine. Kron attempted to escape by dropping to his back. Marcelo countered by stepping over into the mount, keeping the top position and getting the finish.*

Rolling away is an excellent escape for the guillotine choke.

Marcelo countered by catching his back as he rolled, ending in the mount and finishing.

Yes, prepare to win. Learn your submissions. But also prepare for things going wrong at the last minute.

COUNTER ESCAPES: SALES

What do you do when an objection slips through? It will happen from time to time; when you train properly however, you have your own counter moves, your *objection counters*, practiced.

Incentives are one great way to counter objections and prevent "escapes" from the close. A powerful incentive is a sign-now or act-now bonus. Those can take a few forms. There could be an initial discount for "paid in full" or "sign today": you get a discount amount or a percentage off the project. Action today is worth more to you than action tomorrow. If you are prospecting a larger organization, these signing bonuses can mean a fairly big discount *and help the ROI happen even faster*, which may lead to your next deal with them. When it comes down to something that's in the thousands or tens of thousands, even hundreds of thousands of dollars, a signing bonus is a fast-mover incentive, which works great.

The other type of incentives are value-adds, so rather than discount the price, you add on value that does not have hard costs but improves the quality or speed of the project. For example, if it's a creative endeavor like a video production, you could add additional cameras, or additional gear that would make things look or sound nicer. These have an intangible value—add some more editing time and do some more polishing work. They are elements that don't cost hard dollars but add real value in the eyes of the prospect.

If you add a bonus, it should counter a specific objection. Let's say you're selling something like a group coaching program. As part of that coaching, you are bonusing in additional training of some kind that will help them accelerate their results. Perhaps you're bonusing in a couple of one-on-one sessions, for example. You're bonusing in a Facebook group where they can talk with other people who are also coaching clients. If you are selling something that is a product, then maybe it is the implementation part of the product, such as a dedicated person on your team who answers their questions and helps them with implementation. If it's a SaaS product, getting it implemented and trained in your organization quickly is a huge value-add.

Think about the things in your products and services that are the reason the prospect may decide to say no. Then create a bonus that actually counters it. If you're selling an event, for example, the bonus could be rooms and meals. It could even be flying people in to attend. It could involve ongoing support after the event with group coaching or by providing the recordings from the event.

What are the things that will get them to sign? Does it not cost you a lot and counter an objection at the same time? When these things all meet together, you get people to take action faster, it gets you to the yes and the close quicker, and you get happier clients. Incentives will serve them, allow you to get to implementation, and *make them happy*.

I had a vendor partner I approached with a sponsorship opportunity at an upcoming event. They complained that the leads we were sending them were not converting. I offered up a one-hour sales training session with me as a bonus for doing the sponsorship deal. Having an incentive that directly addressed their objection helped close the deal immediately.

ACTION STEPS

Empower your teams with valuable incentives that will counter objections. As a team, think deeply about what these could be. Create a list of incentives and guidelines on when and how to apply them. Remember these value-adds are ultimately to get to a yes quicker. Decide if you're going to create a sign-now, dollar-figure, or percentage discount as a bonus or some other option. A powerful option is a paid-in-full deal package or a special discount price for paying in full. Consider offering multi-installment pricing, with a finance fee to discourage its use. The key here is to have your teams fully understand the playing field they work within.

BREAK RESISTANCE

BREAK RESISTANCE: JIU-JITSU

Once you have limited their avenues of escape and countered any they do attempt, you have the submission fully locked in. Victory is in your grasp, but they are still going to try their hardest to resist you. They are going to use their strength to prevent their arm from being overextended. They are going to flex their neck to try to outlast your grip on the choke.

If a choke is on, it may still take time for the opponent to tap. "Breaking resistance" could mean outlasting them, patiently keeping the choke locked in. If their hands are defending, it could mean breaking through those defenses.

There's a certain point when you are armbarring someone when you can feel their will break. You begin to apply pressure to their elbow. Initially, they try to resist, bending their arm to counter your extension of it. You can feel the tension in their arm. They use their strength to resist it, and then—they give up. They can't stop you. Even if you don't tap them in that very moment, they're no longer resisting with strength. Their resistance has been shut down. That is a critical moment and aim.

It is not always the last moment, but you won't ever get there without this step.

*This is not to be overlooked if we are seeking to actually finish every time. Sometimes sheer will is what holds us back from victory or allows us to push through. "I **will** tap you." There must be an element of this mindset. You can feel it in a match. You can feel when someone's will breaks—and when it won't.*

If you've set up, attacked, and reinforced your submission, the final step is breaking through their resistance. Don't let up; finish the match.

BREAK RESISTANCE: SALES

Some salespeople feel defeated when they're presented with a no or an objection they can't counter. Sometimes a junior salesperson's will is broken in that moment, and they *tap out*. An elite salesperson, however, sees a no as a *no, not now*. A no is not a no forever; it's just a no for today. This speaks a little to mindset. Remember, it's not a no against your solution. *It's a no against them fixing their problem.*

You've done everything in your power to show them that you can solve this problem. And they're still saying no, or they're countering the idea of solving the problem. This is simply a defense mechanism against admitting that there's a problem or going through the pain of solving it.

Remember the brain wants to keep itself safe. It will try to keep us out of pain, creating excuses to not solve a problem.

And while this can be challenging, our job is to have a steel will to win the fight. The resistance that you're getting needs to be systematically broken back down again. Focus on the fact that they're deciding to not solve the problem. Then redirect them back to the problem and the urgency around it. Make the problem the focus, not their counters to your solution.

I was working with a pharmaceutical company that had created a drug and drug protocol to help stroke victims gain more maneuverability in their day-to-day lives. The team developed it, did the research, and had the clinical trials but weren't getting the traction within the organization to get money to start marketing the drug and the protocol.

It was a family-run business in a big market. The major stakeholders needed to really feel a story about the people the drugs were helping. Their marketing lead approached us for a solution to create a video. The goal was to encompass the story of some success cases in a compelling way to open up more funding internally. It wasn't an externally used video; it was for an internal department to show the stakeholder.

Our marketing lead had a hard deadline for the meeting with the stakeholders and he wanted the video done to a high quality. It takes both money and time to do this the right way. We needed to show the right amount of pre-stroke history of that person, so you felt for them.

It was going to require a good investment even though it was for an internal piece. The resistance was the budget. It was really big for an internal project. The client said, "I don't know if I can justify the cost." The counter was "Do you want this to go anywhere? Because you can have this shot in a couple of months. [Future casting] If we don't sign today, we're not going to have it done in time."

At the end, I simply said, "Let me help you on this path, and let's circle the day to remember that you made this decision that will help so many lives." And he said, "F*ck yeah, let's do it."

Some senior reps do not break the resistance. It takes heart and grit to push. I have seen some reps say, "You let me know what's happening, and I'll check back in with you next week." *No!* Fricking go for it; go hard! Make it about the things that matter to that person.

Help them recognize how important what they believe is and what they are doing is and that it's okay to aim for excellence.

ACTION STEPS

Role-play some recent sales scenarios that could have been an opportunity to break prospects' resistance but were missed. Map those conversations out and find the things that could have been said that would've broken their resistance. Now establish your own will-breaking database and add updating it to your SOP. You can download an example of that database at www.salesjiujitsubook.com/resources.

CHAPTER 9

WIN

This is the end of the line. Again, some opponents will have tapped already. Only the toughest will stay in the game this long. This is our final step in making sure we tap everyone and seize the victories we've earned. It requires disciplined persistence—even a bit of ruthlessness. This is the professional's game. Master this and dominate. Remember, the best way to serve the opponent is by doing everything we can to win. This is **taking that task seriously**, carrying the weight of **being a professional** and having the discipline to **cement** things until victory is *officially* yours.

SHOW YOU'RE SERIOUS

SHOW YOU'RE SERIOUS: JIU-JITSU

If attempting to finish the submission was your first stab at ending the match, this is your last. All the elements are in place for you to win if you haven't already. You attacked. You prevented and countered their escapes. You overcame their resistances and broke their will. Now it's on you to convince them it's over.

*In the 2010 Ontario Open fight where I landed in mount after attacking the armbar from the bottom, I attacked the collar choke to get the opponent to defend, and I slid up to S-mount. He knew he was in danger of the armbar **and** the choke. I attacked the choke and, as he bucked wildly, I took the armbar.*

The speed and manner with which I fell back could have caused serious damage and he got ready to tap. Seeing his hand about to tap and how tight the armbar was, the ref stepped in to stop the match. The opponent hadn't quite tapped, in part because I was being nice in order to avoid breaking his arm and so everyone froze for a second.

*The armbar was on—I was in the finishing position. It was out of consideration that I was trying not to hurt him and going easy. Seeing that there might be a possibility of losing this position and opportunity, I bridged my hips up into his elbow, causing him to tap. My being "nice" could have cost me the fight. It wasn't until he **knew** I was serious that he tapped.*

Ronda Rousey, an Olympic judo medalist, began fighting MMA in 2010. After a few amateur wins, she went pro in smaller MMA shows. She quickly rose through the ranks due to the unparalleled level of her skill. She would simply clinch and throw everyone (a specialty in judo). She had an incredible armbar game. With such an exciting champion to spotlight, the Ultimate Fighting Championship (UFC) began a women's division, with her headlining the debut event. Her opponent, Liz Carmouche, was a tough fighter with many submission wins of her own and a pro record of 8-2.

Early in the fight, Caramouche, escaping one of Rousey's attacks, actually jumped on Rousey's back. After nearly catching a rear naked choke, she lost position. Rousey threw her off and stood above her, eventually getting back to her favored hold down, where she hit Caramouche uninterrupted. Eventually, after a near escape from Caramouche, Rousey established a juji gatame—"cross-body hold down"—a position synonymous with the armbar because it is the exact position from which you armbar someone.

*As soon as she established the position, Rousey prevented Caramouche's defense by holding one of her legs. Instead of trying to use a hitchhiker escape, which grabbing the leg prevents, Caramouche did a sit-up escape. Rousey **countered that escape** by spinning underneath, flipping Caramouche over, back into the juji gatame, the armbar position.*

After stopping all of the escapes, Rousey still had to deal with the fact that Caramouche had grabbed her own arm, preventing Rousey from extending it. While Rousey tried to break the grip, Caramouche started bucking wildly. Rather than lose the position by fighting to finish, Rousey opted to get back on top to a more secure spot from which it was easier to counter the defense. Peeling Caramouche's hands apart, Rousey was able to lie back with the arm extended, though Caramouche was still holding on. Arching back, first the grip broke, then Caramouche's resistance, and almost immediately Caramouche tapped out because Rousey kept on attacking, never letting up on the pressure from her bridge. She was serious about her bad intentions toward that arm, and Caramouche could feel it.

Keep in mind that all of this is happening in the blink of an eye. It looked simply like Rousey lay back, broke the grip, and finished. But that's because there was no let-up from Rousey. She persisted to the end.

With pressure, you let them know that you will follow through if they don't tap. If they don't believe that, they will be far more emboldened to keep fighting. They must understand that the threat of going to sleep or the arm being broken is real, so that they understand the magnitude and tap. Notwithstanding, a crafty opponent may let you think they have given up just to lull you into a false sense of security in your victory. Do not fall for it; follow through. Finish them.

You have won the match. But it doesn't always end here. Make sure it does.

SHOW YOU'RE SERIOUS: SALES

It's time to *win*. The cost of inaction (COI) is one of the greatest closing tools you have. You've already hit them with the ROI, which is obvious. "It takes X amount more new clients or efficiency to pay for this. You'll have fewer people leave you. You'll have more clients, etc."

What you haven't hit them with is "What is the cost of *not* making a decision to work with us? What are the repercussions?" As you're hooking them into this final moment of yes, you may need to bring this out as a tool in your toolbox, to further push them into the yes. This is very much an intuitive moment to use this tool. Keep in mind you don't always need to use this particular tool. It's a tool that, even though you've passed a resistance, might be the next piece that you need to put in place to seal the deal. The COI is the cost of them not taking action and working with you. What is the cost of not implementing your solution to solve their problem? Remember, we asked these questions back in Reinforce, where we future-cast what would be possible when this problem was solved. Now you simply repeat that back to them exactly as they told it to you.

What happens if this problem is left unattended, not solved? What is the impact on their business, their income, or, depending on the type of product, even their personal lives? What is the impact on their employees? What is the impact on their mission? What is the impact on their clients? Think in a global sense; what are the repercussions of not solving the problem?

Sometimes that cost is tied to a new initiative, and this may not be as relevant. If it's solving a problem that is persistent already, there's already been an impact, but this is also looking at the future impact. What is the future impact on the business of not solving the problem? This future vision paints the picture of the problem as a clear and present danger that needs solving.

When implemented correctly, this is a salient moment, a waking moment. For many businesses, it comes down to core functions that can't continue properly without this problem getting solved.

We worked with a manufacturer who did metal fabrication. They had some amazing statistics: their error rate was less than about .01 percent—crazy low, as if errors don't happen.

On paper, they almost sound too good to be true—until you go into their facilities, and see how well set up it is, how clean it is, how every station is organized, how everyone cares about what's going on, how the entire organization is aligned. The problem they were having was that quality was too often overshadowed by price.

Everyone just wants the cheapest price. But if you get the cheapest price, and a quarter of the stuff is wrong, what's the cost to your assembly line if that needed part is wrong? Or if you are building a building, and you're on the fiftieth floor, and you get a part that doesn't fit, what is the cost on those other businesses? What was the cost of not using their firm and dealing with the error? The problem we needed to solve for the metal manufacturer was "If you have to compete on price, yet you're high in price because of the quality that you provide, then you're losing business. You're losing business every day, which means you can't keep the quality you want. You talk about your employees as family, and you may have to lay off some of your family. You may have to downgrade some things."

There's a cost to them. There's also a cost to their potential clients who would benefit from working with them; if they simply understood the difference a few extra cents makes, they would see the value. We created an amazing video, which actually spoke to this. "Yes, we're more expensive, but here's why. When you look at the big picture, we're actually *less expensive* because our defect rate is so low and our accuracy is so high. If you calculate the time that you put into installation, in getting the wrong parts that don't fit versus having everything perfect the first time, you'll see that the difference is worth the extra money."

ACTION STEPS

Do a review of your recent clients and figure out what the cost to them would have been if they had said no to working with you. Now that you are delivering the product or service to them and both you and they have seen the benefit, deep-dive and critically think about the impact of your product or service. What was the emotional impact? How much money could they have lost? How many clients could they have gained or lost? You see the benefit. What would have been the cost to them of *not* implementing with you or taking on your product or service?

You know how much money they're gaining, or how much market share. What you don't know are those other intangibles. Now that they're a client, you might be able to ask those questions. "How much more money do you think you've made since we've implemented our product, or how many more clients chose to renew this year with you?" Think about questions that are directly related to your product or service. Get the data. Once you have, catalog it in a COI catalog you'll share with your team. An example of the headings to use to create your COI catalog can be downloaded at www.salesjiujitsubook.com/resources.

THE PROFESSIONAL'S BURDEN

THE PROFESSIONAL'S BURDEN: JIU-JITSU

*If you've gotten to this point, you've shown that you will really follow through on the submission, whether it be putting the opponent to sleep or hyperextending or over-rotating a joint. If they still have not tapped, it is time to **actually** follow through.*

*In the finals of the 2014 IBJJF Women's Black Belt Featherweight world championship between Michelle Nicolini and Tammi Musumeci, Nicolini was down on points with just a few minutes left. A master of spider guard, Nicolini used it to catch Musumeci in a unique armbar with her arm caught all the way behind her back. Almost immediately, Musumeci's arm bent backwards, dislocating. A warrior, Musumeci refused to tap, knowing she was winning. Many would have released the arm, but a professional and a warrior herself, Nicolini continued to attack, using her shin to try to hyperextend the arm further. Unable to move, but tough as nails, Musumeci **still** did not tap. Unfortunately for Musumeci, her bravery was for naught, as Nicolini was able to use the remaining time to get on top, finishing with an eventual 13–6 score.*

Nicolini, despite Musameci's arm being dislocated, stayed on the attack.

Jiu-Jitsu is typically an incredibly safe sport because generally people tap when they get caught in submissions. As we have seen, though, they don't always. In these cases, we have to follow through. It's the warrior's obligation. You have to do it if the opponent gives you no other choice. If they present you with that situation, you must follow through. It's not pleasant, but we're professionals. And we're here to win.

THE PROFESSIONAL'S BURDEN: SALES

You've hit them with the cost of inaction. Now, the logical brain should be satisfied. Keep in mind there are two types of decision makers. There are emotional decision makers and there are logical or tactical decision makers. Salespeople often sell how they like to buy. In other words, they are only using one kind of closing tool.

An emotional sales rep, who buys things on emotion, may say, "Trust me. Buy it. It's going to feel good." The person will say,

"Well, okay, but what am I getting?" "Don't worry about it. It's going to feel great!" The logic-based sales rep may say, "Here are the features and benefits. It's going to give you this, and it's this much, and we're going to come in on Tuesday, and we're going to be able to install the new server, etc." The logical seller is going to get into all of those features and benefits and never talk about the emotional aspect as to why they should buy and the emotional feelings around solving the problem.

It's the sales rep who does both who ultimately will have greater wins. At this point in the process, we switch to playing on the emotional element of the sale. Eighty-five percent of the people will make a decision based on a gut feeling, on an emotional basis. Some of the logical people will have already made the decision not to buy, and regardless of what you say here, it won't move them. Your leverage is with the emotional buyers; you want to be able to hit them with that emotional feeling at this point.

Your excitement about solving their problem is what allows you to trigger their emotions. It becomes an exciting prospect to get the problem solved. Be excited and ask them to allow you to help them. Say to them, "Let us help you solve this problem. Let us get you started on the journey. Let us get this dialed in to your business. Let us help you help others. Let us play a small role in making your dream come true. Let us help you make your impact."

After reinforcing and encouraging your client's vision, tie that powerful emotion back to the fact that they have already decided to solve the problem. Remind them that in deciding to go forward, they had the courage to take the action necessary to make the dream a reality. This moment allows your team to ultimately close at a higher rate.

I spoke to a lady who was thinking of investing in a workshop that I was selling. She said, "I'm retiring and I want to do something; I just don't know what." For more than forty years, she'd been an educator of educators. Think about that for a minute. What a noble and underappreciated profession. Teachers are already underpaid, overworked, and undervalued in our society, and here's somebody who had impacted thousands of educators and the next generation of kids. Those kids could be the next leaders, the next parliamentarians, the next statesmen and stateswomen.

Then she said, "Well, I want to do something different. I'm really into energy healing right now."

I said, "Wait a second. You've had an entire lifetime career, your entire adult career working in one university teaching these educators. You're an educator of these new teachers; you were educating them to go off and be teachers. What was special about what you did?" I asked her to tell me one story that proved to her that she had a profound impact.

"Well, my specialty was teaching them different ways of teaching some subjects that would engage kids in exciting ways with topics like math and English, using different techniques."

"Wow, okay," I said. "Give me an example of how you impacted some of your students."

"Oh, well, yeah, just yesterday, one of my student teachers came up to me and said, 'You know, ma'am, I've actually always struggled with this math concept, and I was kind of worried about teaching it, and I've got to thank you because today was very healing for me. I actually understand it and now I feel that I can go teach it.'"

I said, "Hello! That is amazing!"

She said, "I'm tired of teaching."

Then I hit her with an emotional point. I said, "What legacy do you want to leave on this earth?"

She started crying.

I asked, "Are those tears of truth or are those tears of shame? Tell me what is going on for you."

She said, "They're truth."

I said, "You were put on this earth to do more than just energy healing on people. You have a gift of helping educators teach kids, a new way of thinking about a core thing like math. That is a real gift. You need to give it not just to the thousands of people you've taught at your university. You have the opportunity to impact a hundred thousand people by going and doing this in other states. Let that be the legacy that you leave. Let us help you." This had nothing to do with logic or money. It was about legacy, something bigger than her.

I said to her, "Let us help you leave a legacy that you're going to be proud of in this world."

Sometimes people resist the thing that they deeply wish they had an answer for. If you can find out what that hidden wish is and present your solution as the path to it, you can create a powerful way to get the emotional close. Maybe you're a coach, or an author, or you're trying to help people reach another level of understanding, or start a new business, or go on a journey that leads them to self-discovery. Maybe you're helping people publish books; maybe you're helping people create or market their product. For many people it is not about the money. Money is a measure of the impact that you make in this world; others just want to make an impact. Knowing when it's about the money and knowing when it's about the impact, and having your team be able to pivot between those two, is a very powerful skill to have as an elite salesperson.

Once you pass the emotional side, it now comes back to logistics again. Now this is where some sales teams make it so freaking hard to actually transact. You spend all this time trying to close them. You get them to say yes, and then you put all these barriers up and make it tough for your sales folks to actually close a frigging deal. You need to make it easy. You need to make *pricing*, *agreements*, and *payments* easy.

Make it easy to get started right now. List the bonuses, any discounts, and all of that stuff. Agreements should be easy to grab, fill out, and get signed—a deal should be easy to implement and get going. If you don't have all of these things dialed in, then you have a problem. You need to make it easy, so fix it now for your team.

ACTION STEPS

Ensure that the actual engagement documentation, and the process of doing the engagement legally, is easy. Ask what the absolute bare minimum documentation would have been necessary to effectively close and transition your last five clients. Make sure that your sales team understands decision makers' emotional triggers for your niche. They'll be different for everyone. Begin to incorporate this element into your role-play.

CEMENT

CEMENT: JIU-JITSU

Once you have earned victory, there are minor hidden missteps that might prevent you from the ultimate win. This is the final level of professionalism.

This whole engagement was about getting the tap. You went through all the steps. You engaged on your terms, you created the opening, you seized the opening, you improved your position, you set up a submission, you attacked the submission, and you reinforced it. You prevented and recountered all counters. You broke the opponent's will; you came close to putting them to sleep or breaking their arm or leg.

They tap.

You let go right away.

The ref didn't see it.

Now what?

What if the opponent denies it? Are you leaving it to their good character to say yes, they tapped? We might hope everyone is of strong character, but even if that were the case, who knows what they are even conscious of while pumped so full of adrenaline?

*In these rare cases, you **can** leave it up to the opponent's integrity. And that will lead to some percentage of victories.*

In the 2010 IBJJF Pan Championship in Long Beach, California, I fought an opponent who pulled guard on me in the middle of the match. He used the "Kiss of the Dragon" technique to spin between my legs, attempting to take my back. I immediately pounced on a toe hold, his foot cracked, he screamed out (a verbal tap), and I let go.

Attacking the "toe hold" ankle submission as the opponent tried to spin under me.

The ref came over to stop it and separate us. The opponent denied having tapped. The referee, having heard him tap, argued with him briefly, but the opponent insisted.

Not sure what to do, the ref walked off to consult the head ref and then awarded me another two points and restarted the match. I ended up winning anyway, but it cost me four minutes of energy.

In 2003, few outside of Brazil had heard the name Marcelo Garcia. At the ADCC World Championship, he was an alternate who, in the second round, faced another legend who was expected to win the whole division, Vitor "Shaolin" Ribeiro. After only a few seconds on the feet, Marcelo attacked with a lightning-quick arm drag, immediately taking Shaolin's back.

Moreover, he already had him in a choke. Within seconds, Shaolin had been put to sleep. Rather than let go, Marcelo held on and kept squeezing until the ref came over, confirmed Shaolin was out, and forcibly peeled Marcelo's hands off.

The armdrag allows you to get behind the person instantly.

*Marcelo is known to be one of the nicest guys in Jiu-Jitsu, but on the mats, he is a ruthless professional. There is little worse in this game than winning and having it not count. The tap is not enough if you want every win to count. Keep going until the ref stops you. You must **keep** the victories you've earned.*

CEMENT: SALES

Having a win not count is one of the nightmare scenarios of a sales rep. You do everything and you get the yes, and the next day's buyer's remorse kicks in and you get a phone call asking to cancel the deal.

A hidden decision maker said no. Or the next day the now sober client says, "You know, we're just not comfortable moving forward." This is like a tap not counting. In sales, it's so important that you finish the conversation a certain way after a yes so that this does not happen to you.

Many just take the yes and run out. Do you take the yes and take them out for dinner? Maybe. But after you get the yes and payment has been arranged, you now need to mark the day in some way; they need to know you and your organization have their back.

The elite salesperson cements a yes into a *permanent yes*. It's critical to celebrate the decision and to lay out the journey of engagement. It's a cop-out for a sales rep to say, "Well, that's operations. I don't really know about that. They'll be in touch with you."

That's what opens the door for people to cancel. What is the journey they will now go on? This cannot be a mystery. For example, if you were doing a consultancy, the next step is to book a strategy session with the leadership team to determine the best implementation of the consultancy.

You need to lay out the next steps in detail. "The next step is you're going to get an email, which sets up a date for our operations team to come out and talk to you." Or "You'll have an account director who's going to be your liaison, so let's schedule the kick-off meeting with all of us now. I want to tell you what to expect over the next few weeks."

Or even if you're selling a digital course online, you can say, "The email leads you to the course. It gets you your passwords. And you'll start on a course. And we have an amazing team that can answer questions for you." Whatever it is, just give out the details to eliminate any anxiety around the unknown.

Whatever the steps are, you need to frame them for your new client so they understand the journey. They understand the engagement process, versus just signing and walking out the door.

Finally, you're solving a problem. You helped your client identify the problem, see that you can help solve it, and *decide to take action*. This is a day to be celebrated! Have them remember the day by circling it in the calendar: this is the day they decided to solve the problem.

Depending on the kind of product that you're selling, the language here needs to shift appropriately. If you're selling something that's personal to the new client and helps them achieve a dream, you need to help them honor that. "Listen, nobody can take that dream away from you. We have now, together committed to achieving your dream. You have decided to invest in this solution to have your dream of a new business, or a new endeavor, or a new invention come to life. And we are here to support you, but first we want to honor the fact that you've taken resourceful and intelligent action toward solving these problems to turn your dream into reality."

If you're selling at a higher corporate level, you *still* want to celebrate in a way using language that will resonate with your caliber of clients.

Oftentimes, this takes the form of saying, "This might sound a little cheesy, but I would love to just take fifteen minutes and give you a little mini onboarding welcome celebration. I want to talk about the six best things to know about what the next six months are going to look like. Then I'll answer any other questions you've got, see how else I can help to make sure this is a rock-star success. And if it helps you, we can even do this on a semi-frequent basis throughout this process, even though that's not necessarily something we've discussed."

This is not something I can give you my scripting for, because it always changes. It's based on the culture of the individual that I'm selling. It will change if I'm selling to someone in the United Kingdom or Australia or Canada or the United States. It'll change within niches. It'll change to match personalities. Whatever form it takes, it's vital that you cement your new sale by ensuring the client feels great about their decision and that the transition to the next step in their experience is clear and seamless.

ACTION STEPS

Write out the last five people you've closed. How could you have celebrated them in a way that matched both their circumstance and their personality? How would you have used this thinking to make their post-sale experience clearer and smoother? Create a close-cementing script to codify the ways you help ensure new clients *stay* clients.

PART IV

POST-FIGHT

Learning *is not attained by chance, it must be sought for with ardor and attended to with diligence.*

—ABIGAIL ADAMS

This is where the real winning happens. Any individual fight may or may not go our way, but how we **level up** from each experience determines our long-term and ultimate success.

If every stroke of genius and error on the mats can be recorded, interpreted, and integrated, then every battle makes us stronger. Our likelihood of winning the next battle we face depends on how much we have learned from the last one.

This is the masterwork. This is the road from winner to champion.

CHAPTER 10

LEARN

Your job after a battle is to translate experience into insight. Experience is a powerful teacher, but there is experiencing and then there is studying and learning from that experience. What did you learn? How will you change your game and your approach?

Learning begins with having a learner's attitude—**staying hungry**. Then we have to apply that attitude by, win or lose, performing a **postmortem** and then, finally, **integrating** it into our training.

STAY HUNGRY

STAY HUNGRY: JIU-JITSU

After a win or a loss, it's easy to get tied up in the emotion of the experience. It's important to step back and be a student. Be a scientist. Be hungry to get better, whether you've won or lost. Don't get caught up in satisfaction or dejection.

One of my Purple Belts, Amear "Prince" Bani, recently fought a Black Belt in an MMA match. He dominated the Black Belt, making him quit in under two minutes.

It would have been easy to get complacent because it was such an easy victory. Rather than just celebrate though, we asked, "What can we take away from it? What can we learn?"

*There was a moment early in the fight when the opponent shot in for a takedown. He immediately got countered and was forced to the bottom, but the plan had been for my student to stay out of range so it wasn't **possible** for him to shoot. Why did he get to our hips? It's great that he responded well, but it shouldn't have happened in the first place. Even though it was a win in practically every moment, we still had to ask what we could do better.*

Look for where you can improve.

*Jiu-Jitsu is the art of improving by facing challenges. But that improvement isn't a given; it has to be earned—**after the match**. Earn it, win or lose.*

Don't become complacent with a win or dejected by a loss. Use both as fuel and as a chance for a systems upgrade.

Even when you win, look for where you can improve. That's the champion's mindset.

STAY HUNGRY: SALES

Many sales teams have systems in place to learn from a no, but it's rare to see an organization that actually focuses on what they can learn from a *yes*. This is one of the biggest lessons one can take away from Jiu-Jitsu: the idea of learning from wins as well as losses.

It's a very rare organization that focuses on learning from the yes. If you're already doing it, lean into it. We tend to celebrate a yes with a gong, or a horn, or a big email that goes out. "Yay, you made your quota that week, month, or quarter!"

But *just* celebrating the win and never analyzing it is a lost opportunity. In the analysis of what's working, consider two parts.

First, let's acknowledge what you did right, so you can keep doing it. Then figure out what you didn't do right, even though you won, and track it.

The second part is, even though you won, what were elements of the conversation that didn't go as well as they could have? I so love this concept; nothing goes perfectly, but you can learn from even small mistakes. Even though it was a yes, you still had areas you could have improved. For example, did you skip a part of the process? If so, why?

When approaching the review, remember that critical analysis must be emotionless. This will sharpen the sword and help hone your team's focus, attitude, and learning.

Ultimately, your sales reps want to make more money. A rep who's not hungry to make more sales is not a good rep, right? If they're hungry, then they will want that opportunity to learn from the yes.

Give them that opportunity.

Likewise, if your sales force is on the phone or doing video calls, you've got technology to help you audit the yes and the no.

Record for review. If many of your meetings are done in person, you might want to be able to record them in a more covert way for training purposes—not, of course, breaking any privacy laws. The best way around this is to get in the room with them. Go with your reps to those meetings and sit in as a support person. The ability to give them critical feedback in real time will accelerate their growth and learning.

This is about increasing closing percentages. Without this in your SOP, you'll be doing your reps a disservice. They won't get better. Make sure they review and learn.

This review goes both ways: I ask my team to send me two calls to review each week, one miss and one win. They must tell me three things they did correctly with each call and three things they must improve, or I will not watch them. The time they spend watching and thinking critically will reinforce their learning, and *you* will learn how they think, which will help you as a leader to train them better.

A team will only improve their results if they're regularly taking steps forward every week.

Once, years ago, my team had a little bit of a slump. My first instinct was "Darn, I missed call review two weeks ago. Maybe I could have caught something," and I put it on myself. I went in and did a random poll of calls and saw that, on average, they were dropping Sales Kuzushi that week. Simple fix. I didn't have to go chastise them. I just did a new training session with them, a refresher on Sales Kuzushi, and all of a sudden, sales picked back up again. It was a quick case of diagnose, address the issue, reinforce it, continue.

Have an SOP around how many calls per rep that either you or your directors review. Be sure that a couple of them get brought up to you, depending on how flat or deep your organization is.

Provide call feedback in an unemotional way, in a data-driven way that helps the rep close more often.

ACTION STEPS

Take the last five clients who signed with you and break down the entire sales process to find what the rep did well and what they could have improved. Do the same for the last five opportunities that did not close. Use the Sales Jiu-Jitsu Call Review Feedback Template and provide the structured feedback with timelines for improvement. You can download the template at www.salesjiujitsubook.com/resources.

POSTMORTEM

POSTMORTEM: JIU-JITSU

A learner's mindset is fundamental to maximizing the value of each match, but it is not enough. Some lessons will be obvious; some won't. Establish the process of consistently and systematically reviewing your fights and asking what could be done better, and you will see how you can make impactful changes that you might otherwise not come across for years. This accelerates your learning and your chance of success next time. But it is an active process. You must schedule and participate in it. You inevitably learn from experience; this is not that. It is critically analyzing and trying to understand where you were strong and where you were weak.

One of my Brown Belts, Denis Beenen, fought a wily competitor at the 2016 No-Gi Pans as a Purple Belt, losing to him by points. During the match, the opponent used the Kiss of the Dragon from reverse De La Riva guard to take his back. He ended up going on to win the division. Denis was disappointed because he felt he could hang with and beat him and could have taken the division. Denis won the division the next year but didn't end up facing the opponent until Brown Belt No-Gi Pans three years later.

While at first it was discouraging because Denis felt he didn't have an answer for the opponent's attack, doing a postmortem allowed us to really diagnose the issue. The Kiss of the Dragon is a dangerous move from a sport Jiu-Jitsu perspective and difficult to stop—if you don't have an answer. Slowing the footage down, we workshopped a way of shutting down the attack that seemed to work in training.

They met again at the 2019 No-Gi Pans in California at Brown Belt. The opponent immediately pulled reverse De La Riva guard and began attacking with the same game. Sure enough, he went for the Kiss of the Dragon. Using the strategies we had developed, Denis shut it down, a scramble ensued, and they restarted. Denis pulled guard and attacked a sweep. He not only got on top, but as he did, he caught a guillotine choke. With one of the most deadly guillotines I've ever felt, Denis was able to finish this very good opponent.

Our job is to turn losses into lessons. But not just losses—or wins. Did you track your warm-up, your preparation, your mindset, between-fight rest, etc.? The king's game is to learn from every aspect of the fight.

POSTMORTEM: SALES

I often refer to the postmortem as digging for gold, because this is the kind of data that creates innovative *ahas*, innovative approaches, innovative lessons that turn feedback into more sales. If you want your team to get better, review their calls. Do it on a consistent basis. Do it without fail. Foster a culture of openness to that feedback. Get curious about what they were thinking when they made a mistake, as opposed to being accusatory or judgmental. Understanding how a rep thinks allows you to train them better. Don't psych them out or shake their confidence. In review, celebrate what they did correctly and treat the things that they messed up on as opportunities for improvement.

Shaking a rep's confidence in themselves is a disservice to them and your organization. You don't want to beat them down. You want to raise them up and get them excited with additional training. By helping them with a different way to phrase something or a different way to present it or a different way to think about it, you're actually giving them an opportunity to make more money. That's what it should be about. You're helping them be more successful. They keep their jobs, the company keeps money flowing in, and ultimately, they're going to get more *money in the bank.*

Go back to the very beginning of this process. Understanding your rep's why is important. Do they want to buy a new car or take the kids to Disney World? Do they want to treat their spouse to a nice vacation? Whatever it is, whatever they're using extra commission money toward, share in that dream with them so that it's a motivating factor—*in the postmortem*, as you're giving the feedback. You're selling them on the future of their success. When you know their why, you can use that to motivate them. It's plain and simple. You're using the Sales Jiu-Jitsu System to develop your team's skills. *That's* Jiu-Jitsu!

Most reps, often dejected by a no, will be scared to ask a prospect why they decided against moving forward. But that's because they don't understand that this information can enable us, unlike in a Jiu-Jitsu match, to actually turn a loss into a win.

I had an opportunity to work with Canada's largest cable company on recruitment videos for hard-to-recruit positions. A couple of them were sales and call-center positions. We pitched them—a good pitch that solved a really good problem. Then they decided they were going to potentially put the project on hold.

I said, "Well, why did you decide to put it on hold?"

"Oh, our internal team might be able to do it. We can't spend external money when we can play internally."

"Oh, makes total sense."

If I hadn't asked why, I would have thought they said no to me.

It had nothing to do with me. It had everything to do with the internal workings of a big organization.

The next thing I did became a ninja hack for me for years, because it opened up a whole new line of thinking, in terms of positioning, which was Positioning for Number Two. I turned to them and said, "Not a problem at all. It was a pleasure to get to this point of giving you this scope of work. We'd be happy to be your number two anytime. We'd be happy to come in last-minute for anything you need. Pick up the phone. We're here to help. We really enjoyed coming up with the project with you, and we'd love an opportunity to work with you in the future."

A month later, we got a call to come in on a last-minute job. The director of their division needed to do a message to the troops, and they wanted it shot on-brand and shot at their level, so the brand people came in and said, "Here's how we have to do it. Here's how it has to look." We honored that 100 percent. We came in; we over-delivered the piece to them. They loved it. Wouldn't you know it? The original project was back on, and they wanted to use us. They had full confidence, so much so that the creative department were the ones that encouraged them to use us.

What was my next hack? Gratitude. I sent them a gift with a handwritten note. I sent the head person a gift, just thanking them: "Hey, I really, really appreciate it. It means the world to me that you guys recommended us, and here's a small token of my appreciation, just to honor that you did that for us." We did the project, and they loved it. At the end of the project, three months later, the head of the division called back and said, "We've got another project for you. It's going to have to take you through Christmas, but it's $100,000 and it's video for a major sales rally that we're doing for all our sales reps. They're coming in in January, we need all these video assets, and our internal team can't do it. You know, it's a big project for us, and we trust you to represent the brand properly." We won the project.

Then I sent a gift to their entire creative department: lunch on me. Asking why, Positioning for Number Two, and showing gratitude all came up from doing postmortems on sales scenarios and sales situations. These techniques would never have been developed and honed if I didn't do the due diligence of constantly analyzing the yeses and the nos.

ACTION STEPS

If you don't already have postmortems in your SOP, add them. As well, if clients say no, make sure your reps are finding out why and Positioning for Number Two. What does that look like for you? Think of your last five prospects who said no and consider how you could have Positioned for Number Two. Maybe even go back to those clients now, ask why, and set yourself up to turn them around down the line. Also, figure out a gifting policy to show gratitude and to honor the people who refer you. I like handwritten cards and a physical gift shipped to their office. Your current clients are the greatest source of additional sales. You can download our gift idea database here—make sure to add your own after every engagement! Visit www.salesjiujitsubook.com/resources.

INTEGRATE

INTEGRATE: JIU-JITSU

Learning that's not remembered doesn't make a difference. Insights not acted on don't change anything. To truly cement the value of the lessons we learn from our postmortems, it's important to integrate them into our training. These new insights and growth become the new history and inform the future in our next pre-fight phase—and so the cycle continues.

*Black Belt is the highest belt in Jiu-Jitsu and the highest level of competition. That said, my world silver medal was in the masters' Black Belt division—thirty and over. Believe me, the monsters in that division are skilled and tough as nails, but the peak of the sport is **adult** Black Belt—eighteen and older Black Belts. The "true" world champions are the ones who win that division.*

*One of my top competitors, my first Black Belt, Dan Davis was fighting in the 2017 No-Gi Pans, lightweight adult Black Belt. He ended up facing a big name in the sport, Renato Canuto. One of the benefits of facing a big name is you often have **key data**. Renato is known for being one of the most athletic, agile, and acrobatic competitors out there. If you let him move around without controlling him, he will probably pull out some surprise ballistic move as he has done to some of the best in the world.*

Pulling guard to get to one of his most dominant positions, Dan was able to tie him up, not only slowing him down but actually keeping him on the defensive. Constantly off-balancing, Dan attacked a sweep and, as Renato defended, Dan wrestled up. Renato turned away to catch his balance and Dan jumped on his back. Renato was standing up, with both of his arms trapped by Dan's legs, Dan's hand under

Renato's chin in perfect position to choke. As Dan took his back, they went out of bounds and the ref—I believe mistakenly—restarted them in a neutral position, only giving Dan an advantage—worth less than a point.

*To be fair, it was actually Dan's mistake for relinquishing the back when the ref stopped them, rather than **cementing** the position and submission. This would have pressured the ref to either reset them in the same position, give Dan his four points for the back, and/or give him two points for his opponent running out of bounds. But the real lesson was still to come.*

It would be easy to feel as though, against such a high-level competitor, you "lost your chance," having been so close to finishing them, but Dan kept his head in the game and attacked with one of the submissions we came up with while troubleshooting after an earlier fight. Dan got the attack but wasn't quite able to finish and ended up losing on points. Renato not only went on to win the division but the world championship that year too.

In our postmortem, we saw that Dan's attacks were actually working but got stifled with a certain defense. Troubleshooting, we came up with a counter.

*Despite Dan being a full-time lawyer, we would train twice a day, almost every day, getting up to train at seven o'clock in the morning, drilling our new strategies, then testing them in the evenings with our competition team. Dan went on to use these innovations to take bronze at the no-gi Brazilian Nationals, beating some of the best Black Belts in Brazil, and winning gold at the Toronto Open. Once you glean insights from your postmortem, make sure to **integrate** them.*

Post-fight is simply a new cycle of pre-fight. Think of the fight as training, which gives feedback on the game plan we went in with. Postmortem is troubleshooting that helps us hone and enhance our game plan—which we will test again in the next fight.

*You will have more fights. Leverage your learning—integrate it into your training, grow without limits, and continue to **win**.*

INTEGRATE: SALES

Training can't be something that's done once at onboarding and never done again. You want your sales teams to be better, to be more efficient, and to win more often than they lose. You need training to be a standard operating procedure in your business. If your reps are always in a fight and never analyzing, taking the lessons learned, and integrating them back, putting them into your databases, they just won't grow. A database that's never referenced is worthless.

Have the discipline to make the space and time in your week—and month—to put those training reps in; allow for growth, advancement, and mastery. Take the lessons learned and integrate them into your training. That's what it takes to turn a six-figure company into seven, then into eight and beyond.

This is what separates the amateurs from the professionals, the recreational competitors from the elite competitors.

This book is for the elite professional. Black Belt salespeople. Take what you and your team have learned and use it to make everything you do better. Grow.

ACTION STEPS

How do you integrate integrating? Add it to your SOP. Quarterly, ask how your training and systems have evolved because of what you've learned in sales engagements. If you don't measure it, you can't manage it; if you don't schedule it, you won't measure it.

As your reward for having gone through this book, use the link below to download the Sales Jiu-Jitsu System master map—the complete Sales Jiu-Jitsu process checklist—the exact same process we follow in the How to Sell the Sales Jiu-Jitsu Way digital course. We've broken down all the lessons of this book and the course into a simple checklist for you to use when auditing your standard operating procedures, your sales process, and your training procedures so you're able to see both where your gaps are and how to fill them. Download at www.salesjiujitsubook.com/SJJSystem.

CONCLUSION

Plan, fight, win, learn—*repeat*. As you can now see, Sales Jiu-Jitsu is not a set of tools, it's a *system*. Any single component can improve results. Implement them as a whole and change the game. Make it an *algorithm*, a routine you inject into the lifeblood of your business, and watch your success spring geysers of wealth and impact. These are hard-earned lessons, garnered from nearly fifty collective years in Jiu-Jitsu and sales, that can help accelerate your path to ultimate success on whatever scale and to whatever impactful end matters to you (again—to be able to easily integrate the entire system, download the complete Sales Jiu-Jitsu System checklist here: www.salesjiujitsubook.com/SJJSystem).

There are many books designed to get you and your sales organization to a high level, but there are very few for the *already* high-level person and company to take their business to the elite level. Because Jiu-Jitsu is a real, visceral, physical combat system, the processes for achieving success are just easier to see. The Sales Jiu-Jitsu System is a wealth of proven real-life sales conversion architecture that will exponentially increase your sales team's closing rate. It gives you an algorithm for creating, ensuring, and repeating success. We wish you clarity, determination, and *follow-through*. We look forward to seeing you shine.

While it is a complete system, you are not starting from scratch. Don't treat this book as an all-or-nothing thing. Yes, it's a cohesive process and every element of the system works together to reinforce itself. That said, if your team is already strong in one area, start by focusing on the area where they need the most improvement.

Once that is working well, look at the elements within the next area that will have the greatest impact on your sales team. Trying to do a complete overhaul overnight won't serve anybody. By rolling out elements of this book over time, you will see dramatic improvements in the confidence, competence, and success of your sales teams. Your individual sales reps will thank you for these skills. Making this book mandatory reading for them would be a good first start.

Taking the resources (which you can download at www.salesjiujitsubook.com/resources) and doing the exercises *as a team* will ultimately give them a sense of ownership over the process and outcomes, and encourage fast implementation. The resources are meant to help you quickly take action, so you don't have to think about how. They're our gift to you.

We want to see you succeed, and we look forward to hearing how you have implemented the lessons in this book. Feel free to drop a line at success@salesjiujitsubook.com.

And we welcome those readers interested in exploring and embracing the actual practice of Jiu-Jitsu. You don't need to do Jiu-Jitsu to understand the principles in this book, but it will give you a deeper appreciation. To feel what it's like to be working against another human being challenges you in ways you can't imagine. And you will see how much deeper your understanding goes as you embark on this journey.

For a free intro to Brazilian Jiu-Jitsu video course (normally valued at forty-nine dollars), visit the secret link on Elliott's virtual academy, www.BJJ101.tv/free-primer-download.

ACKNOWLEDGMENTS

ELLIOTT BAYEV

Thank you to:

My parents for believing in and supporting me.

Daniel Gellman and Pat Folliott for giving me my start in business.

David Barnett, Bobby Ziner, and Simon Benstead for their friendship, guidance, and mentorship over the years.

Professor Shawn Williams for his amazing instruction and support on and off the mats.

Rickson Gracie, Marcelo Garcia and Eddie Bravo for the inspiration.

Daniel Moskowitz for believing in me and my teaching.

Jayson Gaignard for introducing me to Daniel and so many wonderful entrepreneurs.

Mastermind BJJ member Andrea Palmer for suggesting the idea to Daniel and me.

My brother, Jorge Blanco, for the constant example of relentless hard work.

And of course, all of my students, friends, training partners, and supporters at all of the amazing OpenMats across the world.

DANIEL MOSKOWITZ

First of all, to my amazing wife, Lara, you always believe in me, and that means more than you can ever know. You've pulled me back from dark days and kicked my butt when I needed it. You hold the fort at home when I am gone on the many days for work, and to support this book—thank you! You are my best friend, and I love you more with the passing of each year, and here is to another twenty-four years together with you, my love!

For my amazing children, Hyla and Samara, who are so supportive and encouraging, you might understand this better years from now, but one of the reasons I wrote this book was for legacy. For passing down my wisdom to both of you. Jim Rohn says one of the greatest gifts you can leave your children is your wisdom. So this first book is the professional wisdom that I have collected so far. I may or may not write other books, but it was vital for me to get this done.

Remember what I have taught you to prepare you both to be amazing women, and read this to understand the art of selling, as it's a foundational skill that will serve you both well in all areas of your life. I love you both so very much.

My biggest fan, my father, Willie Moskowitz, as I said in the dedication. Thank you for always pushing me to be the best version of myself. You have been so supportive of this book, pushing me to get it out into the world faster and staying on me so I would complete it.

Thank you for being another proofreader; it was a great help to have a keen outside eye on the book.

To Pete Vargas, thank you for being my mentor and for having me be part of your leadership team. You model for me in so many ways what it means to be an awesome husband, a fantastic parent, and a courageous leader. It's been an amazing journey so far, and I am so excited to move into this next phase of Advance Your Reach's explosive growth. Thank you for your support of the book; it means the world to me.

To the entire staff at Advance Your Reach, thank you for being the excellent Dream Team you are and thank you for your support.

I would like to thank my co-author, Elliott, who has been an excellent co-author, and without his talents and skills, this book would not be possible. Thank you for saying yes and going on the journey with me. I do not care what anyone tells you; writing a book is hard work. We pulled this off while both of us are SO busy with our daily lives, so thank you for putting in the work with me and looking forward to what the future holds for us with this book's success. Thank you, my friend!

Finally, thank you to anyone who ever was on a sales call with me, regardless of whether you purchased something or not. Thank you for all the lessons you taught me. I would not be here without you. My goal is to always leave people better off than when I found them, selling with love, integrity, and gratitude.

ABOUT THE AUTHORS

ELLIOTT BAYEV

Elliott is a lifelong martial artist, having practiced various arts for more than thirty years, Brazilian Jiu-Jitsu for the last twenty-four.

He has been competing since 1998, and in those twenty-plus years he has won multiple Canadian championships, earning the opportunity to represent Canada at world championships in both Abu Dhabi and Poland, as well as competing at the open world championship in California, where he took silver in the 2013 IBJJF No-Gi World Championship Master Black Belt division.

After focusing on business for a few years, Elliott returned to competition in 2017, taking silver at the No-Gi Pans and double gold at the 2017 Rickson Gracie Cup in New York. In addition to his own competition career, Elliott has coached Canadian champions, junior-belt world champions, and world-class Black Belts, medaling at the biggest competitions in Brazil and across the world, and acted as assistant coach for the Jiu-Jitsu International Federation's (JJIF) team Canada in 2018.

In addition to his competitive achievements, Elliott is recognized as a world-class instructor, having taught for the last fifteen years, and founded one of Toronto's longest-running and most successful martial arts academies, OpenMat Mixed Martial Arts, producing champions of his own and, more important to Elliott, changing many lives of "average folk" who train for fun, fitness, and self-defense.

Elliott recently released BJJ courses for absolute beginners just getting started, new students/White Belts who want their Blue Belt, and instructors and school owners looking for effective teaching tools. These courses are available on his new learning platform, BJJ101.tv, as well as on his blog, UnderstandingJiuJitsu. com.

Outside of martial arts and business, Elliott is a philosopher, writer, and systems-thinker focused on uplifting people everywhere. He is the founder of GlobalUnity.org, a movement working to bring the world together.

* To get free access to Elliott's intro to Brazilian Jiu-Jitsu course, The BJJ Primer, visit www.BJJ101.tv/free-primer-download.

DANIEL MOSKOWITZ

Daniel has been in sales for twenty-five years, ever since he was duped by a salesperson and became determined not only to never let it happen again, but to understand what strategies and techniques they used to get him to a desired result so effectively. Thus began his journey of studying the best practices and high-percentage strategies that lead to sales success.

In his long, successful career, he has worked in multiple B2B businesses and professional services industries, personally generating well over $30 million in B2B sales and heading up teams generating tens of millions of dollars per year. He has been responsible for selling key services to Fortune 500 companies, mid-size companies, and local regional businesses.

In 2016, he started his own sales consultancy, working with multiple clients and consistently doubling their sales results. As his business began to take off, he went on a personal weight-loss journey, losing 102 pounds in seven months, and he is now a sought-after speaker inspiring audiences, motivating them around sales and his weight-loss journey.

He has uncovered, created, and developed high-percentage, high-performing strategies, tactics, and techniques that have enabled exponential growth in the organizations he's helped. Currently, Daniel is director of sales at Advance Your Reach, a company that helps individuals, entrepreneurs, and organizations leverage speaking on stages as a major client lead source. Over two years, Daniel helped to grow the organization from a seven-figure into an eight-figure privately held company.

Made in the USA
Monee, IL
20 January 2021